WHAT HAS THE EU EVER DONE FOR US?

HOW THE EUROPEAN UNION CHANGED BRITAIN – WHAT TO KEEP AND WHAT TO SCRAP

DAVID CHARTER

Biteback Publishing

For Kim, Leo and Mikey, with love

First published in Great Britain in 2017 by
Biteback Publishing Ltd
Westminster Tower
3 Albert Embankment
London SE1 7SP
Copyright © David Charter 2017

ISBN 978-1-78590-185-0

10 9 8 7 6 5 4 3 2 1

A CIP catalogue record for this book is available from the British Library.

Set in Minion Pro

Printed and bound in Great Britain by
CPI Group (UK) Ltd, Croydon CR0 4YY

CONTENTS

PREFACE

Reg: They've bled us white, the bastards. They've taken everything we had, and not just from us, from our fathers and from our fathers' fathers ... And what have they ever given us *in return*?

...

Xerxes: The aqueduct.

...

Reg: Oh, yeah, yeah. They did give us that.

...

Masked Activist: And the sanitation!

...

Matthias: And the roads...

...

Another Masked Activist: Irrigation...

...

Reg: All right... but apart from the sanitation, the medicine, education, wine, public order, irrigation, roads, the fresh-water system and public health… what *have* the Romans ever done for *us*?

Xerxes: Brought peace?

Reg: Oh … Peace … Shut up!

– *Monty Python's Life of Brian*

INTRODUCTION

Britain's vote to leave the European Union was nothing short of a revolution. It usurped the Prime Minister, smashed the Cabinet, upended government policy, sent the pound plunging and changed the destiny of the country. The facts got trampled underfoot. The establishment view was overthrown. Above all, however, it was a democratic revolution. British voters chose by 51.9 per cent to 48.1 per cent to quit the EU on a turnout of 72.2 per cent – higher than at the five previous general elections – with 17,410,742 casting their ballot to leave.

On one level, it was obvious what the majority voted for on 23 June 2016. The referendum asked 'Should the United Kingdom remain a member of the European Union or leave the European Union?' Beyond that, many questions – including Britain's new relationship with the EU and the fate of all its rules and regulations – were left unanswered. This book looks at key ways the EU changed Britain and asks in each case what could happen next. It investigates whether the changes would have been made by Britain if it had not joined the European club; whether the measures proved helpful or harmful, effective or unnecessary; and what scope national legislators have to reconfigure the legal landscape following the return of national control. 'What has the EU ever done for us?' is not just an important historical question. It is the basis for asking what kind of Britain we want.

The referendum result set in train the several overlapping phases of Brexit – unstitching the bonds of membership and settling the bills, creating a new deal between Britain and the EU, and deciding how the UK should run affairs previously agreed in Brussels, Luxembourg and Strasbourg. Theresa May, the Remainer who took on the task of leading the country out, quickly launched her vision of a 'Global Britain', with the aim of making trade deals around the world. Closer to home, the return of legal sovereignty meant the British government would revisit laws and practices in numerous areas. As May told the Conservative Party conference in 2016:

> Whether people like it or not, the country voted to leave the EU … We are going to be a fully independent, sovereign country, a country that is no longer part of a political union with supranational institutions that can override national parliaments and courts. And that means we are going, once more, to have the freedom to make our own

decisions on a whole host of different matters, from how we label our food to the way in which we choose to control immigration.[1]

A referendum day poll of Leave voters by Lord Ashcroft found that 49 per cent said the biggest single reason for wanting to quit the EU was 'the principle that decisions about the UK should be taken in the UK'.[2] One third (33 per cent) said the main reason was that leaving 'offered the best chance for the UK to regain control over immigration and its own borders'. Only just over one in twenty (6 per cent) said their main reason was that 'when it comes to trade and the economy, the UK would benefit more from being outside the EU than from being part of it'. Nobody mentioned food labels. It was the core principle of the Vote Leave campaign – to 'take back control' – that attracted voters. The details would have to follow.

May also outlined in that first speech as leader to her party conference that a 'Great Repeal Bill' will remove the 1972 European Communities Act which took Britain into the original European Economic Community (EEC). It will also adopt every European measure which does not already have a basis in national law, leaving legislators in Westminster, Holyrood, Cardiff and Stormont to keep, adapt or scrap former EU rules over the coming years. Critics said it would be better named 'the Great Download and Save Bill'.[3] While 'directives' made in Brussels required a national law to be made to implement them, there were around 12,000 EU 'regulations' which applied directly from Brussels and were not written into the British statute book. Without the wholesale incorporation of these direct laws, exiting the EU would overnight wipe out a multitude of regulations governing everyday practice in aspects of national life from abattoirs to zoos.

The repeal of the 1972 Act will also end at a stroke the most fundamental change in national affairs made by EEC membership: the handing of ultimate legal authority over various policy areas to a supranational administration and its court of judges. The notion of ceding sovereignty over matters dealt with by Brussels was spelled out as far back as 1962 in a pamphlet by Harold Macmillan explaining his government's decision to make Britain's first application to join:

> It is true of course that political unity is the central aim of those European countries and we would naturally accept that ultimate goal. But the effects on our position of joining Europe have been much exaggerated by the critics. Accession to the Treaty of Rome would not involve a one-sided surrender of sovereignty on our part but a pooling of sovereignty by all concerned, mainly in the social and economic fields.

Over the years, successive treaties expanded the policy range of the EEC as well as its membership and weakened the ability of individual countries to block measures by making most decisions subject to a qualified majority vote, meaning Britain had to muster support from a group of allies if it wanted to head off a policy proposal.

There were just nine member states and a limited range of centralised powers when Britain joined the EEC in 1973. It was a step that required some fundamental changes to national life, such as adopting Value Added Tax and new systems of regional funding and farm support. Sovereignty was pooled on policies including fishing, trade and, increasingly, the environment. Focusing on Europe also cemented the shift away from traditional trading partners which had begun with the post-war collapse of Britain's imperial power. The UK opened up to the free movement of European workers, just as Europe welcomed ours – one of the four freedoms which formed the cornerstones of the Common Market, along with the movement of goods, services and capital.

More changes were to come as the EEC developed into the European Union through the Maastricht Treaty of 1993. The powers of Brussels broadened to cover a range of domestic fields including social and employment rights, while all those holding the nationality of a member country were created EU citizens with new rights to settle across the union. The Lisbon Treaty of 2009 further deepened EU controls by ending national vetoes in forty-five policy areas from energy to sport. The extent of European influence over national life was hardly foreseeable in 1975 when the UK voted by two to one to confirm its membership of the EEC. Official government literature for this first referendum emphasised the power of ministers to veto measures not considered in the national interest, but this ability was soon eroded. Ironically, one of the main steps weakening national control was the Single European Act of 1986, which was a priority of the Conservative government of Margaret Thatcher to end restrictive practices and barriers to trade and turn the Common Market into the single market. The price was an extension of majority voting in Brussels, although treaty and tax measures remained subject to national veto. Britain was able to opt out of the euro, as well as the Schengen zone, where passport controls were abolished on member nations' shared borders, distancing the UK from the main Continental adherents of a federal Europe.

It was Tony Blair who best articulated the pro-European case for sharing sovereignty with Britain's neighbours in a speech in 2001:

> I see sovereignty not merely as the ability of a single country to say no, but as the power to maximise our national strength and capacity in business, trade, foreign policy, defence and the fight against crime. Sovereignty has to be deployed for national advantage. When we isolated ourselves in the past, we squandered our sovereignty – leaving us sole masters of a shrinking sphere of influence.

Britain was increasingly defeated on EU policy changes, however. From being on the losing side in 2.8 per cent of votes in 2004–09, it was outvoted 12.3 per cent of the time in 2009–15, more than twice as often as the next most defeated nations, Germany and Austria.[4] Although defeats in Brussels did not always have a big effect domestically, they combined with various rulings of the Court of Justice of the EU (CJEU) – the EU's top judicial body – to contribute to an impression that laws were being imposed on Britain, which was one theme of the Brexit referendum campaign. This feeling was exacerbated by David Cameron's attempt to renegotiate the EU relationship, which reinforced a view of Brussels as inflexible and largely unsympathetic to national concerns. Cameron failed to win meaningful concessions on the free movement of workers, in an exercise which highlighted the limits of national controls over the entitlements of EU citizens.

Beyond the headline topic of immigration, however, one remarkable aspect of the referendum was just how little debate there was about the actual impact of the EU and its laws in other areas of British life. The leaflet sent by the government to every household at a cost of £9 million emphasised the trading benefits of the single market, but barely touched upon the many ways the EU has changed Britain. Now that British politicians will once again be in charge of policies previously set at European level, it is crucial to have a picture of what the EU did and why it did it. As with the hapless People's Front of Judea in *Monty Python's Life of Brian*, who were battling the might of the Roman Empire rather than the consensual Treaty of Rome which founded the EEC in 1957, even the most committed revolutionary might admit there were benefits worth preserving.

Theresa May set out for a 'clean break' in the separation talks with the announcement in her speech at Lancaster House in London in January 2017 that Britain would leave the single market. This gave Parliament a much more extensive role in the future control of British policy than a so-called 'Norway option', which would have meant remaining subject to the 'four freedoms' including the movement of EU citizens as well as numerous environmental and other technical rules.

> Being out of the EU but a member of the single market would mean complying with the EU's rules and regulations that implement those [four] freedoms, without having a vote on what those rules and regulations are. It would mean accepting a role for the European Court of Justice that would see it still having direct legal authority in our country. It would to all intents and purposes mean not leaving the EU at all. And that is why both sides in the referendum campaign made it clear that a vote to leave the EU would be a vote to leave the single market. So we do not seek membership of the single market. Instead we seek the greatest possible access to it through a new, comprehensive, bold and ambitious free trade agreement.

My first book, *Au Revoir, Europe*, published in November 2012, looked at how Britain reached the point of departure from the EU. My second book, *Europe: In or Out?*, first published in 2014 and updated in 2016 for the referendum, contained the arguments on both sides of the debate for assessing how to vote. This book explores some of the most important and high-profile areas where the EU affected British life and looks at what could happen next. It does not aim to be an exhaustive guide to EU actions but to analyse some of the main topics where MPs, MSPs, AMs and MLAs will find themselves busy in the coming years – and some which gripped the popular imagination but which were not quite all they seemed. Theresa May summed up the challenge when she told the 2017 Davos conference: 'Millions of my fellow citizens upset the odds by voting, with determination and quiet resolve, to leave the European Union and embrace the world. Let us not underestimate the magnitude of that decision. It means Britain must face up to a period of momentous change.' This book begins to assess that change, by first looking at how the EU changed Britain.

CHAPTER 1

AIR

Brexit was the word of the year in 2016.[5] At the start of the last century, another newly coined word was on British lips: smog, a blend of the smoke and fog which regularly blighted the industrialised cities. Government did little to ease the conditions that created 'pea-soup' fogs until the Great Smog of 1952. A cold snap in early December that year prompted Londoners to stoke up their home fires, which combined with industrial pollution in damp conditions to create 800 tonnes of sulphuric acid particles. This five-day smog was the worst air pollution event in British history and caused around 12,000 deaths. Sulphur dioxide released by coal combined with nitrogen dioxide, another coal by-product, to form sulphate particles which became concentrated into toxic levels as water in the fog evaporated. After enormous pressure was placed on the Conservative government, it came up with the Clean Air Act of 1956, a milestone in environmental protection law. It introduced controlled urban areas where only smokeless fuel could be burned, along with measures to relocate power stations away from cities. A follow-up Act in 1968 enforced the use of tall chimneys for industries burning fuels to disperse – although not restrict – air pollution. There was no mention of the environment in the EEC's founding Treaty of Rome, but the landmark first summit of heads of government to be attended by a British Prime Minister, in Paris in October 1972, issued an ambitious communiqué in which the leaders 'emphasised the importance of a Community environmental policy' and pledged to set out 'a programme of action'. Britain, however, did not expect Brussels to produce anything much in this field. In 1978, the Department of the Environment advised the European Commission not to waste any time designing green policies because the UK was 'well placed to cope with its own environmental problems'.[6] Today, as Britain plans its post-Brexit future, four-fifths of national environmental legislation derives from EU law.[7] The far-reaching impact on everyday life will be further explored in chapters on energy, farming, fishing, vacuum cleaners and water. This book is organised alphabetically but it seems appropriate to start an analysis of how the EU changed Britain with something as fundamental as the air we breathe.

West Germany was the first European country to set binding air-quality standards in national law amid concern over 'acid rain' killing trees. The European Commission laid down the first laws for all the member nations in 1980 to restrict the very emissions most responsible for the Great Smog. The directive set 'limit values' for sulphur dioxide (SO_2) and smoke particles in a move intended to enhance human health and protect the environment. Brussels claimed its right to legislate came from the need to ensure a level playing field for trade. 'Any discrepancy between ... the various Member States with regard to sulphur dioxide and suspended particulates could give rise to unequal conditions of competition and could consequently directly affect the functioning of the common market,' the directive stated. [8] In 1982, another directive followed to limit the levels of lead in the air, followed by nitrogen dioxide in 1985 and ozone in 1992. In 1996, a directive laid down national assessment and reporting laws, then in 2000, limits followed for benzene and carbon monoxide, and in 2004 legal restrictions were placed on airborne arsenic, cadmium, mercury, nickel and polycyclic aromatic hydrocarbons. Most of the laws were updated and pulled together in a single directive in 2008 on 'ambient air quality and cleaner air for Europe'.[9] With all these new standards in place, the EU began legislating on the sources of emissions. It already had a basic common requirement for car-exhaust testing, dating back to a 1970 directive, and this was progressively tightened in six later rounds of EU vehicle legislation from 1993 to 2014, although 'real-world testing' of car exhausts was not scheduled until 2017, after a prolonged outcry about the way car companies were able to 'game' laboratory tests – more of which later. The EU made the fitting of catalytic converters mandatory in all new petrol cars from 1993 and diesel cars from 2008.

Gases from power stations, refineries and steelworks (SO_2, nitrogen oxides NO and NO_2 – collectively known as NO_x – and dust) were regulated by the EU Large Combustion Plant Directives of 1988 and 2001, requiring companies either to remove pollutants or to opt out of new standards by shutting coal-fired plants by 2015.[10] The biggest number of plants closed was in Romania but the highest electricity generating amount lost was in Britain, which opted out thirteen plants totalling 34.3 gigawatts – around 15 per cent of total UK capacity. Limits for emitting four groups of pollution gases (SO_2, NO_x, non-methane volatile organic compounds, known as NMVOCs, and ammonia NH_3) were first set in 2001 by the EU's National Emissions Ceiling Directive, which set goals for 2010, later revised with tougher targets for 2030. Alongside all this, in 2005 the EU began a mandatory emissions trading scheme for greenhouse gases (carbon dioxide CO_2, nitrous oxide N_2O and perfluorocarbons PFCs), handing out permits which could be sold on if targets were met. Inspired by a call in the Kyoto Protocol for carbon trading, Britain had already launched its own voluntary emissions trading scheme in 2002, which was joined by thirty-four participants. This was phased out as the UK joined the EU system. Cutting greenhouse gas emissions – notably carbon dioxide – across the EU by 20 per cent compared to 1990 formed one of three basic pillars of the EU's overall climate change goals for 2020, known as the 20-20-20 targets, agreed in 2007 and also in-cluding an increase in energy efficiency of 20 per cent and a 20 per cent share of renewables in energy consumption.

All of these EU measures set binding goals in British law for the first time and helped to clean up Britain's air consid-erably compared to the 1970s. Some anti-pollution goals have been set by other international organisations and treaties, but had it never joined the EU, there is evidence that Brit-ain would not have acted as quickly or as extensively as they were obliged to by Brussels. Successive governments dragged their heels and occasionally ended up in court for failing to meet some of the EU targets. The drive to banish lead-free petrol in Europe, for example, was given early momentum by Britain but ended up being led by Brussels. In 1983, a Royal Commission on Environmental Pollution called for 'all new petrol-engined vehicles to be running on unleaded petrol by 1990 at the latest'. The Conservative government accepted the general recommendation but wanted to consult on the deadline and said that change could only be achieved on a Europe-wide basis. It raised the matter in Brussels but in the meantime Austria, Denmark, Finland, the Netherlands, Sweden and West Germany went ahead and banned leaded petrol unilaterally while Britain waited until an EU directive in 1998 set the final deadline of 1 January 2000, with the then Labour government lobbying for an extension.[11]

More recently, under the 2008 air-quality directive, EU member nations were supposed to comply with limits on nitrogen dioxide (NO_2) in 2010, but could extend that to 2015 if they came up with plans to deal with high levels of the harmful gas. NO_2 is mainly produced by diesel vehicles, which were heavily marketed and spread rapidly in Europe under pressure to cut carbon dioxide, because of car industry guidance that more CO_2 was produced by petrol engines. Indeed, such was the intense focus on hitting the EU's main climate change goal for 2020 that the European Commission proudly announced in 2007 that it was replacing its fleet of petrol cars for its commissioners with diesel models, to set an example.[12] Diesel vehicles, however, turned out not to be the solution to cutting air pollution or even greenhouse gas reduction, as suggested by the car industry PR machine. The Department for Environment, Food and Rural Affairs (DEFRA) admitted in 2014 that only five of the UK's forty-three air-quality monitoring zones complied with EU NO_2 levels, with thirty-five expected to be compliant by 2020 and three zones – Greater London, the West Midlands and West Yorkshire – not due to comply until after 2030.[13] DEFRA had previously said the capital would comply by 2025. This failure to clean up city air landed the British government before the Court of Justice of the EU (CJEU) in 2014, when lawyers for the European Commission called the case 'perhaps the longest-running infringement of EU law in history'. This was the same month that researchers at King's College London said they had recorded the world's highest levels of NO_2 in central London. Writing in 2014, Dr David Carslaw of the Air Quality Expert Group explained how

NO_2 levels became so high in Oxford Street, a road dominated
by diesel-powered buses and taxis, and which had the country's highest flow of buses. It is worth repeating in full to show
how the drive to meet one EU emissions target – cutting the
greenhouse gas CO_2 – gave rise to such terrible NO_2 pollution,
which is harmful to human health:

> Most NO_2 in the atmosphere comes from the oxidation of
> nitric oxide (NO) to NO_2 by ozone. Historically petrol and
> diesel vehicle emissions of NO_x (the sum of NO and NO_2)
> have been dominated by emissions of NO ... However,
> over the past ten years or so there has been an important
> change in diesel vehicle emission technology that has led
> to substantial increases in emitted NO_2. The reason is the
> increased use of diesel oxidation catalysts and particle fil-
> ters. To burn off the black soot from diesel vehicle exhaust
> requires temperatures in excess of 500°C, which is a much
> higher temperature than the exhaust gases reach. However,
> NO_2 is a very powerful oxidant and it can be used to help
> burn off these sooty particles at much lower temperatures
> (around 200°C). These emission control systems therefore
> deliberately produce increased emissions of NO_2 to help
> burn off the sooty particles – and they are very effective in
> doing so. High numbers of vehicles with this type of emis-
> sions control technology is at the heart of the high ambient
> NO_2 concentrations seen in London and across many sites
> in Europe.

In September 2015, DEFRA estimated that NO_2 caused 23,500 premature deaths in Britain annually.[14] As a result of the 2014 CJEU case, the Supreme Court in Britain ordered the government to rewrite its plans to meet EU targets. The new plans included clean-air zones to be introduced in Birmingham, Nottingham, Derby and Southampton by 2020, with the owners of the dirtiest buses, coaches, lorries and taxis charged to enter. Privately owned passenger cars, which make up 88 per cent of the British motor fleet, were to be exempt from charges.

The government was taken to the High Court again and, in November 2016, lost again. Judges said ministers knew that over-optimistic pollution modelling was being used, based on unreliable laboratory tests of diesel vehicles rather than actual emissions. The government agreed to formulate an-other new timetable to bring pollution down to legal levels. During the High Court case, documents showed the Treasury blocked plans to charge diesel cars to enter cities blighted by air pollution, concerned about the political impact of anger-ing motorists, many of whom may have believed their diesel cars were 'cleaner' than petrol vehicles. The Departments of Environment and Transport both recommended changes to vehicle excise duty to encourage the purchase of low-pollution vehicles but the Treasury also rejected that idea. The documents also showed that the government's plan to bring air pollution down to legal levels by 2020 for some cities and 2025 for London were driven by the EU – the dates had been chosen because that was the date ministers thought they would face European commission fines. Further proof of Britain's failure to clean up its inner-city air came early in 2017 with the startling revelation that London had breached annual air pollution limits set by the EU just five days into the year.[15] Hourly levels of NO_2 were not supposed to exceed 200 micrograms per cubic metre more than eighteen times in a whole year but this benchmark was passed late on 5 January on Brixton Road in Lambeth.

In 2015, one reason for higher than expected NO_2 levels was revealed when the giant German carmaker Volkswagen admitted to having fitted 11 million diesel vehicles worldwide with software that detected when they were being tested in laboratory conditions and switched the engines to a cleaner mode. Back on the road, they pumped out illegally high levels of fumes. By one calculation, VW cars with so-called 'defeat devices' could have been responsible for between 237,161 and 948,691 tonnes of NO_x every year worldwide.[16] Volkswagen passed EU testing to comply with EU emission levels, including that carried out in Britain, but was caught by the more rigorous US assessment and standards. Concerns had been raised about the misleading levels of exhaust gases from diesel cars recorded in official EU tests for years. Laboratory tests failed to give a true picture of real driving conditions; for example, devices to reduce emissions tended to switch off in colder temperatures, which manufacturers said was necessary to protect the engine. Department for Transport testing in the wake of the VW scandal found none of the top-selling diesel cars met legal limits for nitrogen dioxide on the road, emitting on average six times the permitted levels even though they legitimately passed laboratory testing.[17]

It remains to be seen if the EU's 'real-world testing' regime, due to start in 2017, encourages better compliance by the car companies or more imaginative ways of passing the tests. Britain would be free after Brexit to introduce tougher tests, as in the US, but the evidence suggests this is unlikely – in December 2016, the European Commission began legal action against the UK and six other EU countries, including Germany, which it said failed to enforce rules aimed at keeping dirty diesel cars off the road. 'Germany and the United Kingdom broke the law by refusing to disclose, when requested by the commission, all the technical information gathered in their national investigations regarding potential nitrogen oxide (NO_x) emissions irregularities in cars by Volkswagen Group and other car manufacturers,' the Commission said. Greg Archer, clean vehicles director at Transport & Environment, a campaign group, said: 'National regulators must stop protecting their friends and clients in the automotive industry.'[18] In February 2017, the European Commission sent a 'final warning' to Britain for failing to address nitrogen dioxide levels in sixteen areas including London, Birmingham, Manchester, Leeds and Glasgow. The next step would be to take Britain to the CJEU, but any fines imposed would probably not apply after Brexit, given the government's determination to leave the court's jurisdiction. Jenny Bates, air pollution campaigner for Friends of the Earth, said: 'It's shameful that the EU has to take legal action against the UK government to get it to deal with the dangerous levels of dirty air across the country.'[19]

Despite the leeway given to European car manufacturers, EU measures have contributed to dramatic reductions in some noxious gases. UK emissions of sulphur dioxide – the first pollutant directly targeted by EU law – dropped by 96 per cent from over 6 million tonnes in 1970 to 0.31 million tonnes in 2014.[20] In the same period, nitrogen oxides have fallen by 69 per cent, although DEFRA admitted that 'road transport still accounts for 34 per cent of UK NO_x emissions in 2015 and the rate of reduction from this sector has slowed down due to the increased contribution from diesel vehicles'.[21]

DEFRA also acknowledged the role of the EU's Large Combustion Plant Directive in cutting emissions in Britain:

The 16 per cent decrease in total NO_x emissions between 2012 and 2015 occurred due to similar reasons to those de-tailed for SO_2: the closure of a number of coal-fired power stations meant that emissions from the energy industries fell by 27 per cent over that period which was the greatest change for any emissions source group.[22]

If Britain were to remain in the EU single market following Brexit, it would have to retain all the air-quality and emis-sions laws previously adopted into British law because the original basis for the legislation was to prevent competitive advantage through lower environmental standards. Outside of the single market, however, Brexit brings the freedom to retain coal-fired power stations and ease expensive pollution limits for energy, industry and vehicles. Cleaning up the air is not cheap. DEFRA said in September 2015 that efforts to meet the EU targets had cost 'some £2 billion since 2011 to increase the uptake of ultra-low emission vehicles and cleaner transport, and supporting local authority action'.[23]

The key piece of legislation driving greenhouse gas emissions cuts in the future is a unilateral British government measure – the Climate Change Act of 2008, passed under a Labour government, which obliges the government to cut the six Kyoto gases by at least 80 per cent by 2050, surpassing EU targets. The Conservative government committed in 2015 to phase out all coal-fired power stations by 2025 but attracted some criticism for planning to replace capacity with gas – which has lower harmful emissions than coal – rather than renewables. And despite the British government's initial reluctance to accept mandatory EU air-quality targets, the global environmental movement has gained such momentum over the past four decades that it would be impossible not to retain some pollution goals. Britain signed up enthusiastically to binding emissions targets in the Kyoto Protocol in 1998, committing it to reduce greenhouse gases by 12.5 per cent in the UK by 2012. For the later Doha amendment to Kyoto, the EU offered a general 20 per cent reduction by

2020, less than the 22 per cent already achieved by Britain by 2012. In parallel, Britain ratified EU membership of the UN's Gothenburg Protocol to Abate Acidification, Eutrophication and Ground-level Ozone. Revised in 2012 with stricter targets, Gothenburg requires the UK to reduce sulphur dioxide emissions by 2020 by 59 per cent compared to 2005 and to reduce nitrogen oxide by 55 per cent.[24]

The companies which pollute the air have well-organised and effective lobbying operations, as seen in Brussels whenever the EU tries to restrict emissions or improve testing for vehicles to match real-world conditions. Britain too was often a lobbyist in Brussels against stricter laws. Much of the progress towards clean air stemmed from its EU membership and – despite the diesel vehicle fiasco – leaving will remove an important agent for improvement.

CHAPTER 2

ANIMALS

First developed in the 1930s, battery cages for hens became widespread from the 1960s with the increase in intensive factory farming to produce food more cheaply and efficiently. The battery system of long rows and several layers of cages initially improved hygiene standards, with conveyor belts underneath to carry waste and sloped floors to collect eggs. Artificial lighting and the use of Vitamin D enabled hens to produce eggs all year round, leading to conditions which became more cramped, in barns holding up to 30,000 birds. Brussels first stepped in to introduce minimum standards for battery cages for hens in a directive in 1986, agreed by a qualified majority of countries.[25] Britain voted against. The then Conservative government argued that Brussels did not have the power to use majority voting to set common cage sizes and brought a challenge at the Court of Justice of the EU (CJEU). During the court case, the EU admitted that 'the protection of animals is not in itself one of the objectives of the Community' but CJEU judges agreed with the European Commission that common standards for chicken cages were necessary 'to prevent distortions of competition on the market for poultry and eggs which might result from differences in the conditions in which animals are kept in different Member States'.[26] The directive allowed each hen 450cm^2 of cage space and included a call for a later review based on 'scientific developments regarding the welfare of hens under various systems of rearing … accompanied by any appropriate adjustment proposals'. Pressure grew from animal welfare campaigners for an end to the practice of battery hen farming because of growing evidence that the birds suffered in barren cages by being unable to express natural behaviours. In 1991, the animal welfare group Compassion in World Farming submitted a petition to the European Parliament calling for animals to be recognised as sentient beings capable of suffering, which was initially adopted by the EU as a non-binding 'declaration' but later became a fully fledged treaty article – more of which later. The European Commission's Scientific Veterinary Committee concluded in 1996 that 'it is clear that because of its small size and its barrenness, the battery cage as used at present has inherent severe disadvantages for the welfare of hens'. This led to a landmark new directive in 1999 enforcing 'minimum standards for the protection of laying hens', which set out a ban on barren battery cages across the EU and their replacement with larger 'enriched' colony cages.[27] These gave laying hens at least 750cm^2 each in cages which must be at least 2,000cm^2 in size, a nest, a clawing board, litter for pecking and scratching, at least 15cm of perch and 12cm of food trough. The directive prohibited new conventional cage systems from January 2003 and banned all use of barren battery cages from January 2012, giving producers a generous twelve years to comply. It was incorporated into English law in 2002, updated in the Welfare of Farmed Animals (England) Regulations 2007, and adopted in similar but separate legislation in Wales, Scotland and Northern Ireland. British egg producers spent nearly £400 million replacing barren battery cages with the larger enriched version. While the UK complied on time, the deadline was missed by thirteen member nations and the EU announced court action in April 2013 against Greece and Italy, the last two countries to continue with battery hen cages. Italy was found guilty in May 2014 and Greece in September 2014 of failing to end battery farming, but neither country was fined, merely ordered to pay court costs. 'Some looking at the ruling will no doubt wonder what the point is in adhering to the law if others can break it with what amounts to impunity,' commented Compassion in World Farming.

After the EU ban on veal calf crates, in a 1997 directive which came into force generally in 2008 – many years after the UK's unilateral ban in 1990 – laying hens were the first animals to benefit in Britain from a specific EU law improving their conditions. The general legal framework for all animals was dramatically changed by another landmark measure used ever since by welfare groups to apply pressure to legislators. The British government pushed for the sentience of animals to be upgraded into EU law and it became a protocol of the Amsterdam Treaty of 1999 – a legal recognition not capable of being a basis for new laws – and then fully incorporated into the Lisbon Treaty of 2009 which stated that:

> In formulating and implementing the Union's agriculture, fisheries, transport, internal market, research and techno-logical development and space policies, the Union and the Member States shall, since animals are sentient beings, pay full regard to the welfare requirements of animals, while respecting the legislative or administrative provisions and customs of the Member States relating in particular to reli-gious rites, cultural traditions and regional heritage.[28]

When Britain ratified the Lisbon Treaty, this became the first general acceptance in UK law that animals were sentient beings. At a European level, this contributed to measures for other farmed species, such as the 2013 restriction on individual sow stalls for pigs (which was set out in an EU directive in 2001 following a unilateral British ban in 1999). Britain was also a forerunner of another milestone in animal protection with a ban in 1998 on testing cosmetics on animals, which was not prohibited across the EU until 2009. However, a complete ban on the sale of cosmetics with ingredients tested on animals, even if this was done outside the EU, was not adopted in Britain until an EU regulation banned all such imports from 2013.[29] The European Federation for Cosmetic Ingredients launched a test case in Britain on behalf of three companies which wanted to sell cosmetics in the UK which had been tested on animals for the Chinese and Japanese markets. The High Court referred the case to the CJEU, which confirmed in September 2016 that 'access to the EU market is conditional upon compliance with the prohibition of animal testing … EU law makes no distinction depending on where the animal testing was carried out.'[30] A further piece of farm animal legislation was a 2008 directive on minimum standards for pigs which banned routine tail docking and stated that all 'pigs must have permanent access to a sufficient quantity of enrichment material in order to enable proper investigation and manipulation activities.'[31] It meant that pigs should always be provided with items such as straw, branches and vegetables to enable foraging, but these requirements are often not met and pig welfare remains an area targeted by campaigners for potential improvement post-Brexit.

For animal welfare campaigners, there were other frustrations with EU law. Despite the recognition of animals as sentient beings capable of suffering, the CJEU ruled that Britain could not ban live exports as this would breach EU free movement rules. In a case referred by the High Court over the refusal of the Ministry of Agriculture, Fisheries and Food to ban the live export of veal calves, judges at the CJEU ruled in 1998 that one EU nation could not implement a complete ban on companies trading live animals because this would be a distortion of the common market. They agreed with the British government argument that 'a ban on the export of calves would … affect the structure of the market and, in particular, would have a considerable impact on the formation of market prices, which would interfere with the proper functioning of the common organisation of the market.'[32]

According to the Royal Society for the Prevention of Cruelty to Animals (RSPCA), around 80 per cent of all UK animal welfare legislation originated from the EU through some forty-four different laws. Farm animals are covered by eighteen EU laws setting standards on the way they are reared and produced, transported and slaughtered. Twelve laws cover wildlife, some of them reflecting international treaties. One of the most effective was a regulation banning imports of wild-caught birds, which was responsible for a dramatic drop in numbers brought into the UK from more than 60,000 in 2003 to virtually none after 2006.[33] The UK had no plans to bring in such a ban, which the EU was able to push through as a measure to combat avian flu. The use of animals in research is regulated by nine different laws covering the breeding, care and use of animals for scientific purposes, transport of animals and the use of animals to test chemicals. For pets, five laws provide rules for the free movement of identified and vaccinated dogs and cats. There is also an EU-wide import ban on products made from dog and cat fur, which came into effect in 2009. Thirteen of the forty-four EU laws relating to animal welfare came in the form of directives incorporated into UK legislation, while thirty-one were regulations and decisions likely to be incorporated in British law under the Great Repeal Bill.

Brexit brings both concerns and opportunities for animal welfare campaigners. The general legal recognition of animals as sentient could be lost when the Lisbon Treaty no longer applies in Britain because, unlike EU legal acts and court judgments, it is unclear how a treaty article will be transposed into UK law under the Great Repeal Bill. One measure which could be revisited by a post-Brexit government is the ending of routine six-month quarantine for dogs, cats and ferrets under the EU's programme of 'pet passports', which ensures animals with the appropriate vaccinations can cross borders. 'The UK was very reluctant to get rid of the quarantine of dogs being imported. The law on the free movement of dogs was passed in 2003 but it took until 2012 to implement fully. The UK resisted for nine years and, without the EU pushing, the UK may well still have quarantine,' said David Bowles of the RSPCA.[34] Dogs entering the UK had been subject to a six-month quarantine since 1897 over fears of rabies, but improved vaccinations meant the risk from pets had become vanishingly small.

Although certain EU requirements for animals are perceived by some farmers and food companies as examples of the red tape that Brussels is famous for, Andrea Leadsom, the Environment Secretary and prominent campaigner to leave the EU, has pledged that animal welfare will be a selling point of post-Brexit Britain. 'By cutting the red tape that comes out of

Brussels, we will free our farmers to grow more, sell more and export more great British food – whilst upholding our high standards for plant and animal health and welfare,' she told the Oxford Farming Conference in January 2017. With Britain keen to open up markets with big agricultural exporters like Brazil and Thailand, farmers and welfare campaigners will be watching to ensure that trade deals protect and enhance the UK's generally high standards. Leaving the EU will also lead to a renewed push from the RSPCA and others to have CCTV cameras installed in all slaughterhouses. David Bowles believes that the lack of a clear mandate to require all abattoirs to have camera monitoring in the 2009 EU regulations on 'the protection of animals at the time of killing' has been used by the government to avoid making the measure compulsory.[35] Although around four-fifths of slaughterhouses have adopted CCTV voluntarily, undercover filming at some of the other establishments has revealed incidents of cruelty. The RSPCA also aims to improve conditions for pigs on farms. 'Unfortunately the EU directive on pigs was not clearly written,' said Bowles.

It says that tail docking should not be done except for a veterinary reason but then you have everybody saying they do it for veterinary reasons. On the enrichment side, where it said pigs should have additional manipulative material, in fact what a lot of farmers do is put a chain in the middle of the pen and say that is their enrichment material, even if the pig does not interact with it.

George Eustice, the Farm Minister, said during the referendum campaign that pig welfare could be one area to improve through a new system of incentive payments to farmers under a revamped support policy after leaving the EU's Common Agricultural Policy. 'If animals had votes they would [vote to leave],' he said. 'We could use CAP funds to promote higher animal welfare. There is a growing consumer interest in wanting to know that the chicken or pork they buy has been treated well. There is a strong appetite for policies that would promote that.' He suggested that farmers could be paid a premium for giving pigs straw to forage in and for not cutting off their tails. 'A pig that has not had its tail docked is usually a good indicator that it has been in a high welfare environment. [Paying a premium] would get farmers thinking about how they would get by without tail docking.'

The ban on battery cages for hens seems certain to stay and the larger enriched cages are coming under pressure, with all the major supermarkets pledging that by 2025 they will no longer use enriched cage eggs. 'The retailers are aware of reputational risks of using low-welfare products – we are more and more going to see progress coming from the retailers,' said Peter Stevenson of Compassion in World Farming (CIWF).[36] The group will, however, push for legislation for dairy cows, given the trend towards zero-grazing – the practice of cows being kept continuously in sheds and having cut grass brought to them instead of going out into pasture. 'There is no UK or EU law on dairy cow welfare, which is a big failure given that cows are increasingly zero-grazed,' said Stevenson. This means that, inside the EU single market, even if Britain had unilaterally banned zero-grazing, it could not ban imports from other EU countries of cheese or other milk products from zero-grazed cows. Animal welfare groups will also make a new attempt to end live animal exports from Britain once it is free from CJEU jurisdiction. 'In the late '90s there were 2.5 million animals exported a year – 2 million sheep for slaughter and half a million young calves to be reared as veal. That figure has fallen to 37,000 sheep a year but it is still 37,000 too many,' said Stevenson. The question – with Britain outside the EU single market for agricultural trade – will be whether a unilateral ban on live exports falls foul of World Trade Organization rules. A spokesman for the WTO said that it would only become clear if Britain could ban live animal exports when the precise details of a proposal were known. 'It depends very much on the circumstances,' the WTO spokesman said.

One question that should be asked is, what sort of animals would these be? Secondly, WTO rules permit a variety of measures for curbing trade in live animals including protection of other animals, persons or plants in the importing country. There can be also exemptions including the protection of public morals, protection of exhaustible resources etc. But without specifics on the type of measure taken, and why, it is very difficult to surmise whether any move … would be in compliance with WTO rules. As a general

matter, what is true is that any measure applied would have
to be transparent and non-discriminatory … In the abstract
it is impossible to answer [the] question with any certainty.

The future of farm animal welfare in the UK will largely
depend on two other important themes featured in later chapters: incentives for farmers under Britain's new agricultural
support scheme and the terms of trading relationships with
the EU and further afield. The future of zoo animals is also
dependent on Brexit talks. Britain's Zoo Licensing Act of 1981,
requiring all animal collections to be registered and inspected,
pre-dated the EU's Directive of 1999 on the keeping of wild
animals in zoos and was used as a blueprint for it.[37] However,
the welfare of exotic animals could become more bureaucratic rather than less after Brexit. Zoos fear that the smooth
exchange of rare animals around the Continent for breeding
programmes could be complicated by more red tape replacing
the free movement they have enjoyed under EU membership.
Kirsten Pullen, chief executive of the British and Irish Association of Zoos and Aquariums (BIAZA), said animals with
shorter life spans such as rare types of rodent would be among
the most vulnerable if the free movement of animals was not
re-established after Brexit. Breeding programmes required approximately 200 animals of a wide genetic variety to minimise
any potential inbreeding effects, she said. 'We have to make
sure EU and UK animal health law fits because this is very
important for the exchange of animals for our conservation

and breeding programmes. For example, it was only by coop-
erating with European zoos that we managed to maintain a
European herd of scimitar-horned oryx.'[38]

One recent EU measure has caused a headache for zoos,
however. The 2015 Regulation on Invasive Alien Species was
considered a blunt instrument which banned the keeping of
certain animals across the EU to protect particular areas of
Europe, Pullen said.[39]

> We recognise the need for making sure we do not have inva-
> sive species coming into our habitats and wiping out native
> species. But they [the EU] are hitting zoos and aquaria quite
> hard with a list of species that are no longer allowed to be
> kept. We have licences dealing with keeping animals on
> site and preventing escapes but we are being told we can no
> longer keep coatis [a member of the raccoon family], a central
> American species, because they have a problem with them in
> Majorca. Obviously we have a very different climate and the
> chances of a population becoming established here are very
> slim. It is frustrating because zoos are establishments used to
> keeping animals, while there would be absolutely no way of
> the government knowing if private individuals were keeping
> these animals as pets and releasing them into the wild.

One domestic wild animal likely to lose out from Brexit is
the great crested newt. Porpoises might also be left out in the
cold. That is because the government is considering repealing

the EU Habitats Directive of 1992, which mandated member nations to maintain the 'favourable conservation status' of a wide variety of threatened animal and plant species.[40] Wild birds received their own protections in the Birds Directive of 2009.[41] While gravely endangered in some parts of Europe, the great crested newt remains fairly common in England, but EU legislation set a common protection standard across all twenty-eight member nations. Downgrading the status of newts would help developers wanting to build on their habitats who have been forced to fund costly removal and relocation schemes for the amphibian. John Tutte, chief executive of house-building company Redrow, said the varying seasonal requirements for different species left them 'a very small window' to start construction and singled out the treatment of the newt for particular criticism. 'The UK has the largest colonies of great crested newts in the whole of Europe,' he said. 'We have not got a shortage, there is no threat to great crested newts in the UK, but it is European legislation.' House builders can remove newts to another colony, but Tutte said this was only possible at certain times of the year. 'You cannot collect and transport the newts to new sites if the temperature is below five degrees. So it writes off the winter for being able to do those works on the site,' he said.[42] The habitats directive is seen by some politicians as symbolic of Brussels red tape tying up Britain with unnecessary burdens. George Osborne, the former Chancellor, said in 2011 that it placed 'ridiculous costs on British business', and George Eustice, the Farm Minister, said before the referendum that 'the birds and habitats directives would go ... the directives' framework is so rigid that it is spirit-crushing'.[43] Eustice added: 'If we had more flexibility, we could focus our scientists' energies on coming up with new, interesting ways to protect the environment, rather than just producing voluminous documents from Brussels.' In September 2016, the European Commission launched a case at the CJEU against the British government under the habitats directive for failing to provide safe marine areas for porpoises.[44] The Commission said it had repeatedly urged the government to designate special sites but it had so far only come up with one small area in Northern Ireland and a proposed site in Scotland. Government sources suggested in February 2017 that the habitats directive would be among measures to be repealed after Brexit.[45] One minister said: 'We'll keep most EU legislation in domestic law but there is some – like the laws that protect newts – which we can adapt to fit our national circumstances.' Stanley Johnson, father of Boris, was a former adviser at the European Commission who helped to establish the habitats directive. 'The Spanish have the lynx, the Romanians and Slovenians have wolves, elsewhere in Europe there are bears,' he said. 'I think we should be proud of our great crested newt. I hope this element of EU environment law does not take too much of a pounding.' A government spokesperson said that the UK had a long history of wildlife and environmental protection. 'We are committed to safeguarding and improving these, securing the best deal for Britain as we leave the EU.'

CHAPTER 3

BANANAS

In the canon of classic British tales of meddling Brussels bureaucrats, none has greater resonance than the notorious bendy banana. It is the 'euro myth' that would not die. Born in the early 1990s when the European Commission embarked upon a myriad of regulations to harmonise product specifications in order to facilitate trade for the start of the single market, the bendy banana story quickly became a fixture of tabloid Brussels-bashing. The Eurocrats were banning the 'abnormal curvature' of bananas. It sounded silly and was ripe for puns and double entendres, giving it all the ingredients for a great British joke. It even surfaced in the British referendum campaign when Boris Johnson, speaking at the launch of the Vote Leave battle bus in Cornwall in May 2016, declared that 'it is absolutely crazy that the EU is telling us how powerful our vacuum cleaners have got to be, what shape our bananas have got to be, and all that kind of thing'.

Johnson added that these regulations were part of an array of EU measures 'costing UK businesses about £600 million a week in unnecessary regulation'. The sway that the bendy banana story held over the British psyche was demonstrated in February 2017, when an audience member of BBC One's *Question Time* programme said that she changed her mind at the eleventh hour to vote for Brexit because she spotted a straight banana in a supermarket: 'I was voting Remain and at the very last minute I changed my decision and I went to Leave. The reason … is because I go to the supermarket and a banana is straight. I'm just sick of the silly rules that come out of Europe.' The bananas found at British supermarkets, corner shops and market stalls were, however, not in the least bit affected by the much-mocked 'abnormal curvature' rule, which amounted to a lowest common denominator for standards across the Continent. A series of other EU measures would change the supply of bananas to Britain dramatically – but the bendy banana was a red herring.

The fun started with the publication of a regulation in 1994 'laying down quality standards for bananas'.[46] This stipulated that:

in all classes, subject to the special provisions for each class and the tolerances allowed, the bananas must be: green and unripened, intact, firm, sound; produce affected by rotting or deterioration such as to make it unfit for consumption is excluded; clean, practically free from visible foreign matter, practically free from pests, practically free from damage caused by pests, with the stalk intact, without bending, fungal damage or desiccation, with pistils removed, free from malformation or abnormal curvature of the fingers, practically free from bruises, practically free from damage due to low temperatures, free from abnormal external moisture, free from any foreign smell and/or taste.

With the exception of bananas produced in Madeira, the Azores, the Algarve, Crete, Lakonia and Cyprus, 'the minimum length permitted is 14cm and the minimum grade (width) permitted is 27mm'. The bureaucrat who drew up this innocuous technical guidance for traders must have been taken aback by the *Sun* front page which thundered 'Now They've Really Gone Bananas' and added that 'Euro bosses ban "too bendy" ones and set up minimum shop size of 5.5 inches'. It was a classic anti-Brussels headline, right down to the substituting of beloved British inches for suspicious Continental centimetres. Other papers could not resist joining in, with the *Daily Express* among those printing a cut-out-and-keep EC-size banana for readers. *The Sun*'s own life-size cut-out was provided under the headline 'See how yours measure up'. Nor could the *Independent on Sunday* the following weekend resist a double entendre when it informed its readers: 'It is a fair bet that if bananas were not shaped like penises, they would not have made it quite so big in the news last week.' It added that 'this was a measure intended to protect the citizens of the European Union, not to bully them. All member countries consume bananas and several grow them … These are good reasons for laying down common minimum standards for bananas.' The London correspondent of the *New York Times* observed that:

> The story of the outlawed 'bent banana' is the latest to make the rounds … will it join the others on the 'euro myth list' like the one about fishermen having to wear hairnets as they pull in the catch? Or the banning of Britain's red double-decker buses? All of these were rumours that bubbled up here as the latest regulation to be imposed by the European Union … None of them are true, or entirely true. But they show that anxieties about joining the European Union still run strong and find an outlet in get-a-load-of-this tales that are widely believed and mock the bureaucrats based in Brussels.

In common with regulations for every other fruit, nut and vegetable imported into the EU and traded between its member nations, a regulation was drawn up to set minimum standards for bananas. One of those bemused at the press coverage was Stuart Anderson, who in 1994 was managing director of Geest Europe, at the time one of the biggest European banana import companies. He says that the frenzy obscured the true aim of the regulation – to stop the abuse of cash subsidies provided by Brussels under the Common Agricultural Policy to EU banana producers.

At the time these regulations came in, 20 per cent of bananas coming into the EU were from EU territories – Martinique, Guadeloupe and the Canary Islands. Twenty per cent came from ACP countries [Africa, Caribbean and Pacific ex-colonies of Britain, France and one of Italy] and 60 per cent came from the dollar banana countries, basically Central and South America. The European producers were getting subsidy based on the difference between their price and the dollar bananas, plus a bit more, and that was based on weight. So what did some of these farmers do? They put stones in, they put stems in, and as few bananas as possible. The European Commission did not want the European consumer funding crooked banana growers and decided to bring in minimum standards so they were not just compensated on weight. The minimum standard was way below the standards of any wholesaler or retailer in Europe – a really basic standard. Somehow the British press got hold of it and completely misrepresented what it was all about. This was a regulation to prevent the EU from having to pay massive subsidies to farmers in Guadeloupe, Martinique and the Canary Islands who were putting things other than bananas in their boxes.[47]

British supermarkets already had much more rigorous standards than those in the 'bendy banana' regulation, Anderson said. The 'abnormal curvature' rule was a broad-brush description which prohibited few bananas from entering the market. It was not the details of the regulation but the wider circumstances of the single market which were the real story – and would change the lives of tens of thousands of farmers around the world. The single market came into force on 1 January 1993 and was designed to facilitate the free movement of goods across the EU by ending restrictive trading practices. It heralded the end of Britain's special banana trading deal with its former Caribbean colonies. Since the early 1950s, bananas had entered Britain tariff-free from Jamaica and the Windward Islands – St Lucia, St Vincent and the Grenadines, Grenada and Dominica. The much cheaper 'dollar banana' grown in Latin America was kept out. This meant higher prices for British importers than for those in Germany, whose bananas mainly came from Colombia, but was an agreement able to survive Britain's entry into the EEC in 1973 because France also had preferential arrangements for bananas from its former colonies. These special deals would have been destroyed by the opening up of free trade between member nations unless there had been measures to stop cheap dollar bananas flooding the Continent. So along with its new 'bendy banana' regulation, the EU imposed a 20 per cent tariff on imports of dollar bananas up to 2 million tonnes and a 170 per cent tariff above that level. Soon wholesalers in Germany – the largest national market for bananas in Europe – found the price of their favourite fruit was rocketing. Berlin backed a case against Brussels at the World Trade Organization brought by the Latin American countries which led to some concessions but was to be the first in a series of battles in one of the longest disputes in the WTO's history. It was only finally resolved in 2009 with an agreement to reduce tariffs gradually on the dollar bananas over the next decade.

Success for the Latin American producers at the WTO forced the EU to open up to dollar bananas. An EU free trade deal effective from 2013 with Colombia and Peru reduced tariffs further and in 2016 Ecuador was allowed to join the trade agreement, giving it much lower banana duties by 2020. The implications have been huge for the traditional Caribbean suppliers of the British market. 'Before joining the EU, most of the bananas in the UK came from the Windward Islands, with approximately 85 per cent of the market,' said Leena Camadoo, banana supply chain manager for the Fairtrade Foundation, the UK-based charity working to assist producers in developing countries.

The banana trade in the Windward Islands is smallholder farms and [after the single market] they were having to compete with big plantations in countries like Ecuador and Colombia, so we have seen trade from the Windward Islands completely fall away. Now less than 5 per cent of bananas in the UK come from the Windward Islands. As a result, it has gone from over 20,000 farmers in the Windward Islands to about 500 to 1,000 farmers, so it has had a devastating effect there. It is quite difficult for them to diversify into any other crops because of the landscape.

They are quite susceptible to hurricanes, it is a tropical climate. So there are quite a few people who have gone into the tourism industry or produce crops for local markets but it has been difficult for them to find crops that can be exported easily.[48]

In response to the British tabloid obsession with bendy bananas, the European Commission's office in London tried to put the record, er, straight. 'Curved bananas have not been banned,' it stated in 1994, at the height of the newspaper coverage.

In fact, as with the supposed banning of curved cucumbers, the Commission regulation classifies bananas according to quality and size for the sake of easing the trade of bananas internationally. Quality standards are necessary in order that people buying and ordering bananas can rest assured that what they are getting lives up to their expectations.

The Commission added that 'these standards should improve the quality of bananas produced within the Community. They should thus be able to command a higher price in the Community markets. This should also help reduce Community aid and therefore relieve pressure on the Community budget.' Sadly for producers, prices of the biggest-selling fruit in Britain have been squeezed in the decades that followed. But not because of the 'bendy banana' rule.

At the same time as cheaper dollar bananas were gaining more access to the EU market, bananas became the subject of a fierce price war between British supermarkets which drove down prices for suppliers and exacerbated the switch away from Caribbean to dollar bananas on shop shelves. 'Suppliers say that the UK is one of the worst markets to sell to because we are one of the most stringent in terms of quality and look of the products and yet we pay some of the lowest prices for bananas,' said Camadoo.

Fifty-five per cent of bananas in the UK are sold at a loss. They are one of the most popular items in the supermarket basket. Similar to milk, supermarkets will use bananas to attract people into their store. Retail prices for bananas in the last ten years have halved and production costs have doubled so you see a squeeze on the actors in the supply chain who have their margins cut and less opportunity for investment.

The European Commission was long aware that the EU was ridiculed for the very detailed specifications it set to manage the proportions of fruit and vegetables. It was illegal to sell a cauliflower less than 11cm in diameter, while a small carrot had to weigh at least 8g and a large one at least 50g or measure 20mm in diameter. The Commission attempted to make amends in 2008 by proposing the repeal of 'specific marketing standards' for twenty-six types of fruit and vegetables from apricots to watermelons, and including carrots and cauliflowers. The Commission's press release announced 'the return of the curvy cucumber: Commission to allow sale of "wonky" fruit and vegetables'. Cucumber had become another byword for meddling EU bureaucracy because, unlike the unspecified 'abnormal curvature' banned for bananas, a regulation dictated that Class 1 and Extra Class cucumbers were allowed a bend of 10 millimetres per 10 centimetres of length. Class 2 cucumbers could bend twice as much.[49] Sixteen of the twenty-seven member nations including Greece, France, the Czech Republic, Spain, Italy and Poland tried to block the repeal at a meeting of the European Commission's Agricultural Management Committee. Under a compromise with national governments, marketing standards were maintained for ten other products including apples, citrus fruit, peaches and pears. Each country could, however, exempt these from the standards if they were sold in the shops labelled 'product intended for processing' or equivalent wording. Commodity prices were rising and it no longer made sense to force suppliers and supermarkets to throw away misshapen produce rather than leaving it up to customers to decide. Agreement could not be reached to include bananas in the general repeal of standards so they still had to remain at least 14cm long and 27mm thick in the middle.

The EU's single market hastened the demise of Britain's traditional Caribbean banana trade but Brussels tried to protect it for as long as possible. The decisive factor was the World

Trade Organization's insistence on lowering barriers to the major producing countries. The EU was forced to act by the epic WTO case brought by the Latin American nations and backed by the United States. 'I would imagine that if the UK had stayed out of the single market, trading policies would have changed anyway,' said Camadoo. 'I would very much doubt that today we would be sourcing bananas from one origin only. At Fairtrade we would not encourage inefficient production or try and put producers in a bubble.' Brexit is unlikely to be able to turn back the clock and revive the Caribbean banana industry, even if future British governments wanted to – and whether or not rules on abnormal curvature are maintained.

Six days after his rant at the EU for dictating the shape of bananas, Boris Johnson returned to the subject again on the referendum campaign trail at an event in Stafford. He said:

> If we take back control on June 23 we can also get rid of so much of the pointless rules and regulations that are holding back this country. This gentleman here mentions bananas. It is absurd that we are told that you cannot sell bananas in bunches of more than two or three bananas. You cannot sell bananas with abnormal curvature of the fingers. This is not a matter for an international supranational body to dictate to the British people.

It was immediately pointed out that shops routinely sell

bananas in bunches of four, five or six. Johnson's aides said that he meant to say that bananas could not be sold in twos or threes under the EU regulation, which does indeed state that 'bananas must be presented in hands or clusters (parts of hands) of at least four fingers. Bananas may also be presented as single fingers'. This was not a diktat to retailers, however. A spokesman for the European Commission said:

> This relates to presentation by the trader/importer/packer of the bananas and are thus requirements at trader level (not at retail level). It allows inspectors to do their job efficiently … It is important to be clear here: this rule applies at the stage of release into free circulation (at customs) for bananas originating in third countries; at the stage of first landing for bananas originating in the Union and at the stage of leaving the packing shed in the producing region for the EU bananas. As any supermarket shopper can see, there are no restrictions on the number of bananas in a bunch.[50]

CHAPTER 4

ENERGY

Even as she announced an EU ban on traditional filament light bulbs, Angela Merkel could not resist a joke about the shortcomings of their low-energy replacements. 'Most of the light bulbs in my flat are energy-saving bulbs – they are not quite bright enough, so when I am looking for something that has dropped on the carpet I have a bit of a problem,' said the German Chancellor in March 2007 while chairing her first EU summit, in the days before the creation of a permanent president when national leaders took it in six-month turns to set the EU's agenda. Under her guidance, the then twenty-seven leaders agreed the landmark 20-20-20 climate change targets for 2020, as already mentioned in the Air chapter: cutting greenhouse gas emissions across the EU by 20 per cent compared to 1990, increasing energy efficiency by 20 per cent and boosting the share of renewables in energy consumption by 20 per cent. The imagination of the media was caught by another pledge. 'How many EU leaders does it take to change a light bulb? Answer: 27,' Reuters reported a BBC reporter as saying.[51] In their summit statement, the leaders called on the European Commission to 'rapidly submit proposals to enable increased energy efficiency requirements for office and street lighting to be adopted by 2008 and on incandescent lamps and other forms of lighting in private households by 2009'. A British official was quoted as saying that if every British household were to replace three 60- or 100-watt light bulbs with compact fluorescent lamps (CFLs), the energy saved would be greater than the power used by the country's entire street lighting network. In December 2008, an EU regulation was agreed which, while not explicitly banning tungsten filament bulbs, set increasingly tough power and longevity standards which only low-energy varieties could fulfil, effectively phasing out 100-watt incandescent bulbs from 1 September 2009 and 60-watt bulbs from 1 September 2011.[52] The European Commission declared that switching to energy-saving bulbs across the EU would 'save close to 40 TWh (roughly the electricity consumption of Romania, or of 11 million European households, or the equivalent of the yearly output of 10 power stations of 500 megawatts) and will lead to a reduction of about 15 million tonnes of CO_2 emission per year'.[53]

The ban, when it came in, caused resentment directed at interference from Brussels, and stockpiling of old-style bulbs. The *Daily Telegraph* reported in April 2009 that 'shopkeepers say customers are "panic-buying" armfuls of the 100 watt bulbs, which are becoming increasingly scarce since many supermarkets agreed to phase them out ahead of the end-of-August deadline'.[54] When the 60-watt bulb was banned in 2011, it reported:

> Britons have been rushing out to snap up the traditional bulbs, which shops are allowed to keep selling until their stocks run out ... Kevan Shaw, a lighting design consultant who has launched a campaign called Save the Bulb, said that humans are not physiologically attuned to the type of 'fake' light that the energy-efficient bulbs let out. Humans have evolved with two types of light; daylight in day time and fire light at night time. The warmth and nature of fire light is hard-wired into us,' he said.[55]

The phase-out of traditional bulbs was so indelibly linked with the EU that it featured in the referendum campaign. The actress Liz Hurley wrote: 'If it means we can go back to using decent light bulbs (60-watt, peach-coloured, both bayonet and screw-in) and choose high-powered hairdryers and vacuum cleaners if we so wish, I'm joining Brexit for sure.'[56] Daniel Hannan, the Conservative MEP and Brexit campaigner wrote:

> Why ... should it be up to Brussels to ban traditional light bulbs and oblige us to have the dimmer sort – many of

which have to be imported from China, at great cost to the environment? Why should it be up to Brussels to ban high-power vacuum cleaners, hair-driers, toasters and other electrical appliances? As my wife remarked at the time: 'Never mind keeping the state out of the bedroom, can't you keep it out of the bloody kitchen?' It's not that the EU is necessarily wrong about all these things. But how did we reach the stage where such issues are decided by a Continent-wide bureaucracy and then handed down uniformly to 600 million people?[57]

Including the ban on traditional bulbs in its list of six of the worst rules that Britain will be free from after Brexit, the *Daily Express* wrote that 'widely unpopular EU regulations have restricted the sale of incandescent light bulbs because they were seen as not energy efficient enough. Their more energy efficient replacements – LED and fluorescent bulbs – give off a colder, more unnatural light'.[58]

Like bendy bananas, light bulbs became a byword for EU bureaucratic meddling. And yet scrapping the incandescent energy-inefficient bulb was also exactly what the British government wanted. In its energy review, published in July 2006 – nine months before Merkel's light-bulb moment in Brussels – the Department of Trade and Industry declared:

We will lead a drive to raise basic standards of energy efficiency. Working with other governments, manufacturers and retailers, we will seek to phase out the least efficient light bulbs, remove the most inefficient white goods from the market and limit the amount of stand-by energy wasted on televisions, stereos and other consumer electronics.[59]

Britain was, however, unable to bring in a national ban on tungsten filament bulbs because this would have been against free trade rules under the single market. This was confirmed by Ian Pearson, the Energy Minister, in November 2006, when he said:

> The UK cannot unilaterally ban or prevent the free trade in products such as incandescent light bulbs on the basis of their energy efficiency. However, the government is pressing the European commission to make lightbulbs a priority for regulatory action under the recently agreed eco-design of energy-using products framework directive.[60]

Less than four months later, the pressure paid off and the EU used this directive as the basis for its regulation. The EU banished the incandescent bulb from Britain's homes, exactly as the British government had urged it to do. The Labour government was so pleased that, at the party's annual conference in the autumn of 2007, Hilary Benn, then Environment Secretary, announced that a voluntary agreement had been reached with major retailers to phase out traditional light bulbs even earlier than the EU timetable. 100-watt bulbs would not be generally available from January 2009 and 40-watt bulbs a year later. 'Britain is leading the way in getting rid of energy-guzzling light bulbs and helping consumers reduce their carbon footprint,' he told party delegates. 'Choosing energy saving light bulbs can help tackle climate change, and also cut household bills, with each bulb saving up to £60 over its lifetime.'[61]

The light-bulb revolution was not quite all it seemed, however. Tests by the Swedish Consumer Association conducted in 2012–14 showed that Ikea, Philips, GE and Osram were among companies which exaggerated the energy or brightness performance of their low-energy bulbs on the packets.[62] The discrepancy was caused by manufacturers taking advantage of generous 'tolerances' in official testing procedures for bulbs. The Swedish tests found that a 42W Airam halogen lamp consumed 25 per cent more energy than claimed on the label to achieve its declared 630 lumens of brightness. A GE 70W halogen bulb was 20 per cent duller than its stated 1,200 lumens. A 28W Philips halogen bulb was found to be 24 per cent less bright than claimed, while Ikea's 53W and 70W bulbs both underperformed by 16 per cent. The tolerance loophole was also used by manufacturers of other home appliances such as TVs, water heaters, dishwashers, washing machines, fridges and air conditioners, at a total annual cost to consumers as high as €2 billion a year, the campaign group Coolproducts said. In April 2016, the EU acted to end the 10 per cent margin of error allowed between the advertised and actual energy consumptions of a range of appliances – but excluded light bulbs.[63] This was reportedly due to fears that changing the rules could devastate the light-bulb industry. Jack Hunter, a spokesman for the European Environmental Bureau, said: 'The European Commission is exempting the industrial sector with the strongest evidence of the most serious problem, using a flimsy promise to correct this in future.'

Under the EU directive that required national governments to set non-binding energy-saving targets, Britain set a goal of reducing final energy consumption by 18 per cent by 2020 compared to 'the 2007 business-as-usual projection'.[64] This set precise targets for energy use by industry, transport, households, services and agriculture. Again, this was not seen as European imposition by the Labour government but wholeheartedly welcomed: 'The UK welcomes the focus provided by the Energy Efficiency Directive. As stated in our national Energy Efficiency Strategy, we are committed to maximising the performance of our existing policies and going further.'[65] Besides light bulbs, a raft of new measures were brought in to meet the EU imperative, including 53 million 'smart' meters for electricity and gas (which provide instant readings without the need for an inspector to visit) to be installed in every household by 2020, helped by £360 million in loans from the European Investment Bank. By far the biggest contribution to Britain's energy-saving effort was projected to come from building regulations, which changed dramatically following an EU directive on the energy performance of homes, offices and public buildings in 2010.[66] This required all properties to have an Energy Performance Certificate when sold, built or rented; larger public buildings must display an energy certificate; and all air-conditioning systems over 12kW must be regularly inspected by an energy assessor. The cost of this directive was put at £1.54 billion a year at 2014 prices, making it the sixth most costly of all EU directives, against claimed annual benefits for the economy of £371 million.[67] At the time of writing, Britain's Conservative government was among a group of countries resisting the European Commission's attempt to update the Energy Efficiency Directive to increase the target from 20 per cent energy reduction by 2020 to 30 per cent by 2030.

The other main thrust of EU climate and energy policy entrenched in the 20-20-20 target, along with emissions cuts and energy saving, was the drive for 20 per cent of energy to come from renewable energy sources by 2020. Britain was ahead of the game – the Electricity Act 1989, which privatised generation, also introduced the Non-Fossil Fuel Obligation to require distributors to buy electricity from nuclear and renewable sources. It was superseded by the Utilities Act 2000, which enabled government to impose a 'renewables obligation' on electricity suppliers. Nevertheless, by 2005 renewable energy still only made up 1.3 per cent of its energy mix and under the EU's renewables directive of 2009 the UK agreed to increase that to 15 per cent by 2020 – the biggest percentage increase of any member nation and less than the general 20 per cent goal in recognition of the UK's low starting point.[68] Britain was judged to have met its interim target set across the two years 2013 and 2014 of 5.4 per cent renewable energy, recording a level of 6.3 per cent. But that was still a long way off the final goal. The plan to reach the 15 per cent target was broken down, as the EU required, into three different aims – to source at least 30 per cent of electricity, 12 per cent of heat energy and 10 per cent of transport energy from renewable sources by 2020. Most of the reported progress was made in electricity, with 17.8 per cent coming from renewable sources in 2014, up from 7.4 per cent in 2010. Progress towards renewable energy in transport and heating has been slower, with only 4.8 per cent of energy in both heat and transport coming from renewable sources in 2014. In a progress report on all member nations in 2015, the European Commission warned more efforts were needed if Britain was to hit the final goal. 'Some Member States, including France, Luxembourg, Malta, the Netherlands and the United Kingdom ... need to assess whether their policies and tools are sufficient and effective in meeting their renewable energy objectives.'[69]

The commitment to renewable energy has led to billions of pounds being spent on subsidies for wave and wind power, including through the government's controversial levy on household energy bills. This money was supposed to be capped by the Levy Control Framework (LCF) at a total of £7.1 billion by 2020. But the National Audit Office warned in October 2016 that the larger-than-expected number of wind farm and solar panel schemes commissioned meant it would hit £8.7 billion, meaning a surcharge of £110 on the £991 average annual household bill by 2020, up £17 on what it would have been if the cap was met.[70] The Treasury announced in March 2017 that the LCF would be 'replaced by a new set of controls' that would be 'set out later in the year'.

A report in February 2017 by a former special adviser to Chris Huhne, who was Energy and Climate Change Secretary under the coalition government, warned that Britain was wasting hundreds of millions of pounds subsidising power stations to burn American wood pellets that did more harm to the climate than the coal they replaced.[71] The wood pellets were categorised as 'biomass' and regarded as carbon neutral because the forests from which they came were replanted. The report said that chopping down trees and transporting wood across the Atlantic to feed British power stations produced more greenhouse gases than much cheaper coal. It blamed the rush to meet EU renewable energy targets, which resulted in ministers making the false assumption that burning trees was carbon-neutral. Britain is by far the biggest importer of wood pellets for heat and power in the EU, shipping in 7.5 million tonnes in 2016, mostly from the US and Canada. Nina Skorupska, chief executive of the Renewable Energy Association, defended the practice:

This report hangs on the fallacy that it takes decades for a forest to recapture carbon. That isn't true ... Imagine you have

100 trees, all growing 3 per cent bigger per year. You could remove two trees for timber, with offcuts going to bioenergy, and the forest would still absorb 1 per cent more carbon than the year before. There's no delay involved … Biomass delivers a massive cut in carbon emissions compared to fossil fuels.

The renewable energy directive was identified as the single most expensive of all EU laws in a survey of 100 costliest EU-derived measures by the Open Europe think tank. The recurring annual cost at 2014 prices was put at £4.67 billion, while the benefit to the economy was said to be £333.6 million. The number of jobs in the production of renewable energy more than doubled from 4,200 in 2010 to 10,100 in 2014.[72] While the Labour government had been keen on the original target, the coalition government under David Cameron lobbied hard behind the scenes in Brussels for an end to a mandatory renewable goal after 2020. 'The UK envisages multiple low-carbon technologies: renewables, nuclear and carbon capture and storage, all competing freely against each other in the years to come … For this reason, we cannot support a 2030 renewables target,' the government told the European Commission in 2012, according to a leaked document, which nevertheless called for 'some type of target for 2030'.[73] This was exactly what came to pass. Two years later, when the EU came to revise its 20-20-20 regime for 2030, binding headline targets across all member nations were set for reducing greenhouse gases by 40 per cent compared to 1990 and

27 per cent for renewable energy, while the energy efficiency reduction of 27 per cent was 'indicative'. Each country's new renewable share was left up to them. Pressure led by Britain and France paid off and the Commission decided that 'while binding on the EU, it [the renewable target of 27 per cent] would not be binding on the Member States individually but would be fulfilled through clear commitments decided by the Member States themselves'.[74]

Amid fears that Brexit would trigger immediate backsliding from environmental and green energy goals, the government announced an ambitious carbon reduction target just days after the referendum result. Amber Rudd, the Energy and Climate Change Secretary, accepted the advice of climate advisers and set a target of reducing carbon emissions by 57 per cent by 2030 on 1990 levels in the legally binding 'fifth carbon budget'.[75] 'The government has kept its word to adopt this important target to limit the UK's carbon emissions,' said John Sauven, Greenpeace UK director. However, the status of Britain's renewable energy commitments is more questionable after Brexit. A letter from Rudd leaked to *The Ecologist* in November 2015 showed the private government view that Britain was on track to miss its legally binding renewable energy target by an estimated 50 TWh (terawatt hours), or 3.5 percentage points of its 15 per cent obligation – a shortfall of almost 25 per cent.[76] As it stood at the time, this would have put the government at a double risk of legal action in the UK and of large fines imposed by the CJEU.

In the leaked letter, Rudd wrote to several fellow ministers:

The absence of a credible plan to meet the target carries the risk of successful judicial review, and failing to meet the overall target in 2020 could lead to on-going fines imposed by the EU Court of Justice (which could take into account avoided costs) until the UK reaches the target level.

After Brexit, there will be no ECJ [CJEU] threat. The binding renewable energy targets could be amended or repealed. However, the government's hands will still be tied by Labour's Climate Change Act 2008, which set the toughest binding requirement for cutting carbon emissions of any country in the world, committing Britain to cut by 80 per cent on 1990 levels by 2050. Given the glacial progress on commissioning new nuclear power stations, and equally slow moves to source energy by the controversial process known as fracking, this legislation of entirely British origin would also have to be amended or scrapped to make a dramatic difference to the need for more energy to come from renewable sources.

While the EU cannot dictate the precise energy mix of its member nations, Brexit has highlighted the important influence of another closely related European body over nuclear power. When Edward Heath signed Britain up to the European club at a ceremony in Brussels on 22 January 1972, the pages of the Treaty of Rome and all the laws that flowed from it stood in a pile a metre tall on a pedestal near him wrapped neatly in red tape. What Heath put his signature to was the treaty 'concerning the accession of the United Kingdom of Great Britain and Northern Ireland to the European Economic Community and to the European Atomic Energy Community'. All the debate at the time had been about the EEC, known popularly as the Common Market, but what of the European Atomic Energy Community, known as Euratom? This was one of three 'European Communities' founded in the 1950s along with the EEC and the European Coal and Steel Community, which merged with the EEC in 1967. Euratom remained a separate legal body throughout the development of the EU. Its original aim was to develop a specialised market in nuclear power in Europe, encouraging the safe production of energy, its distribution to non-nuclear nations, security, waste management, and overseeing standards and inspections. Euratom, agreed in 1957, was partly inspired by the excitement surrounding the launch the year before of the world's first civil nuclear power plant generating electricity on an industrial scale – Calder Hall in Cumbria, on the site of Sellafield.

When Britain joined Euratom in 1973, it assumed oversight of the UK's nuclear facilities, responsibility for nuclear agreements with two dozen non-EU countries on the movement of fuel and components, and ownership of all fissile materials in the EU was ultimately vested in the Euratom Supply Agency. Euratom's officials are based at the European Commission in Brussels and, crucially, it is overseen by the CJEU. This last point led the government to announce in its draft Bill for triggering Article 50 of the EU treaties to begin the withdrawal process that it would also exit Euratom. Senior officials in the nuclear industry were aghast. All trading and transportation of nuclear materials by EU countries, from fuel for reactors to isotopes used in cancer treatments, is governed by Euratom. Rupert Cowen, a nuclear specialist at Prospect Law, a London law firm, told a parliamentary hearing: 'If we do not get this right, business stops. If we cannot arrive at safeguards and other principles which allow compliance [with international standards] no nuclear trade will be able to continue.' Lord Hutton, chairman of the Nuclear Industries Association, said membership of the organisation had brought very significant benefits to the UK nuclear industry.

> If we were to leave without having these alternative arrangements in place it would not be possible for companies in the United States, Canada, Japan, India, South Korea, many of our nuclear allies, not least our European friends and partners, to continue to trade with us in nuclear goods and services. This would be a catastrophe for the industry and I don't think we should be under any illusion about that.

He argued for a staged withdrawal from Euratom, warning it would make the task of leaving the EU 'ten times worse' if the UK also had to renegotiate around twenty international nuclear cooperation treaties and securing nuclear fuels. The trick for British negotiators will be to formulate a new relationship which escapes the CJEU – or persuade the government to make an exception in this case.

CHAPTER 5

FARMING

Unbeaten in his fourteen-race career, Frankel became the world's highest-rated thoroughbred racehorse before he was retired after winning the Champion Stakes at Ascot in 2012. He has pursued an active and lucrative retirement back at the 373-acre Banstead Manor Stud at Cheveley in Suffolk where he was born, covering 133 mares in his first season as a stallion at a stud fee of £125,000. That means his breeding exploits earn far more than his lifetime race winnings of almost £3 million. His owner, Prince Khalid Abdullah Al Saud, also receives a nice annual cheque from the European Union. The prince's Juddmonte Farms, owned through an off-shore holding company in Guernsey, was handed £406,825 from the Common Agricultural Policy (CAP) in 2015, most of which was calculated on the size of the land. An analysis of the top 100 recipients of CAP subsidies in Britain that year showed that sixteen were on the 2016 *Sunday Times* rich list and at least one in five were members of aristocratic families.[77] They included the Queen, whose Sandringham estate received £647,528, the Duke of Westminster (£637,709), the Duke of Northumberland (£773,415) and the Earl of Plymouth (£563,845). Farm subsidies are mainly paid on the size of the holding, with a smaller portion of EU funding tied to rural development practices. A total of forty-three farms received more than £500,000 each from the EU in 2015 based simply on the size of their land. There was an attempt by the European Commission and European Parliament to reform the system in 2014 by gradually reducing subsidies above €150,000 a year and limiting each farm to a maximum of €300,000. Britain played a leading role in blocking the limits. In the end, each member nation was required to cut direct farm payments above €150,000 by at least 5 per cent but was given complete freedom over whether to make deeper cuts. Greece, Austria and Poland decided to cap all payments at €150,000 and – because farm subsidies are a devolved power – so did Northern Ireland. Among several countries which opted for higher limits on direct subsidies, Wales decided to cap them at €300,000 and Scotland at €600,000 from 2018. England was among fifteen countries which only applied the minimum 5 per cent cut to higher payments and continued to allow unlimited handouts. 'I do not want to see our successful farmers spending hours and hours with expensive solicitors artificially carving up their holdings to avoid an arbitrary diktat on the size of their holding,' said Owen Paterson, then

Secretary of State for Environment, Food and Rural Affairs. Hannah Martin, of Greenpeace UK's Brexit response team, said: 'It is untenable for the government to justify keeping a farming policy which allows a billionaire to breed racehorses on land subsidised by taxpayers. It is clear that there cannot be a business-as-usual approach to subsidies after we leave the EU.'

Food shortages after the Second World War led Britain and Europe to develop different systems of farm support with the same aim of encouraging home-grown production. The Common Agricultural Policy, probably the most notorious EEC programme, was outlined in the Treaty of Rome and started in 1962. The CAP offered farmers guaranteed prices for their produce through centralised buying up of surplus grain, milk, wine, olive oil and meat to be kept in storage. High import tariffs were set to restrict competition and exports of surplus produce were subsidised. In the UK, farming was regulated by the 1947 Agriculture Act, which set up a system of assured markets and guaranteed prices for key agricultural products to protect farmers and their workers against market fluctuations. The government paid farmers the difference between the market rates they achieved and annually agreed price targets. After Britain joined the EEC, it switched to CAP intervention, which ensured higher prices and encouraged greater production because of the guaranteed buy-up. The British government's last annual price review in 1972 made clear that:

When the common agricultural policy of the EEC applies in full to United Kingdom agriculture, farmers can
expect markedly higher prices for most of the agricultural
commodities they produce … The Government's aim is to
encourage producers to start taking decisions for further
expansion now.[78]

By the 1980s, the policy of intervention was creating grain
mountains and wine and milk lakes. Milk quotas were introduced in 1984 and land 'set-aside' was introduced in 1992 to
subsidise farmers for non-production. Brussels reduced price
support to allow prices to fall closer to the world market rate and
introduced direct payments, paid per hectare of crops and per
head of livestock, to compensate farmers. Payments for wildlife protection and other environmental measures like planting
hedges or trees were introduced from 2000. Subsidy payments
were 'de-coupled' from actual production levels. But despite
successive attempts to slim down the CAP, it still accounts for 38
per cent of all EU spending, with €392 billion earmarked for the
2014–20 budget period, of which €293 billion is for direct payments and €99 billion for rural development.[79] The UK's share
of receipts was set at €22.4 billion for direct payments and €5.2
billion for rural development over the seven-year budget. That
meant nearly 200,000 farmers or landowners in Britain shared
£3.1 billion in 2015 while £5.1 billion went from the UK annual
EU budget contribution to the CAP – a net British subsidy to
Continental farmers of £5.5 million a day.

The EU farm support system is bureaucratic and expensive with numerous different regulations to follow – as touched on elsewhere in this book in chapters on animals and water – along with other measures unlikely to have been devised by the British government outside the EU, such as the three-crop rule described as 'utter madness' by the National Farmers' Union (NFU). This requirement – which was supported by the British coalition government in a vote of agriculture ministers in 2013 – required around 40,000 UK farms with more than thirty hectares of arable land to grow three different crops from 2015. Farms of more than ten hectares were required to grow two crops and small farms were excluded. 'The three-crop rule goes against all of the NFU core policy principles of simplicity, market orientation and increased efficiency,' said Peter Kendall, the NFU president, speaking in 2014.

It will increase costs, reduce efficiency, increase traffic on rural roads and in some cases could lead to negative environmental consequences. By far the vast majority of those farmers practise crop rotation or have built up sustainable continuous cropping systems. They have built their businesses to generate efficiencies, moving towards block cropping, contract farming arrangements and share farming agreements. This rule undermines much of those efforts.

The European Commission defended the move, stating that it

addressed 'environmental concerns related to pressures that modern farming has put on water, soil, farmland habitats and related biodiversity, as well as contributing to tackling climate change'. It added that 'monoculture, for example, reduces soil fertility and increases demand for fertilisers and plant protection products, which in turn can lead to water pollution and harm biodiversity'.

Despite the many annoyances of the CAP, its subsidies have kept hundreds of smaller farms in business. On average 19 per cent of farms in the UK make a loss.[80] Farm income figures for 2015/16 in England show that for two types of activity – lowland grazing and mixed farms – the CAP basic payment scheme prevented the average farm from making a loss. DEFRA said that, across all farm types, the average receipt of direct EU funds (excluding its rural development payments) came to £23,500. Lowland grazing farms were handed £12,900, while their average total income – before staff and all other costs – was £12,000; mixed farms were given EU direct funding of £21,400 towards an average income of £17,900. Cereals farms had an average income of £35,600 including £30,900 from the EU; dairy farms made £42,300 including £20,300 from the EU; and pig farms made £22,000 including £10,400 in direct subsidy.[81] These figures suggest hundreds of farms would have gone out of business without the EU handouts or some kind of support. The CAP has preserved a way of life in many rural areas against the enormous pressures of plunging global commodity prices seen in recent years. No wonder the Treasury's pledge in August 2016 to maintain EU levels of payments until 2020 raised just one cheer from the farming community and has left the future looking very uncertain. Andrea Leadsom, the Secretary of State for Environment, Food and Rural Affairs, probably expected a more enthusiastic welcome for her announcement at the 2017 Oxford Farming Conference that the EU's three-crop rule would be scrapped after Brexit. She also pledged to end more 'rules that hold us back' by banishing EU billboards 'littering the landscape' and 'no more existential debates to determine what counts as a bush, a hedge or a tree'. She concluded that Britain's best days as a food and farming nation lay ahead. 'In leaving the EU, we have been handed a once-in-a-generation opportunity to take Britain forward; a real opportunity to thrive. We can design, from first principles, an agricultural system that works for us.'

Farmers at the conference were in a nervous mood. When Leadsom's audience were asked for a show of hands if they agreed with her that DEFRA was ready to deliver Brexit, the only arm raised was from George Eustice, her Minister of State. The nervousness was not only about subsidies. Farmers need to know what the trading relationship with the EU will be because of their reliance on exports. For example, the Commons Environmental Audit Committee said in January 2017 that about 95 per cent of UK sheep exports went to the EU which could be subject to the basic tariff of 12.8 per cent plus €171.30 per 100kg, depending on how talks went with

Brussels (see Trade chapter). Britain's farmers could also lose out from new trade deals with non-EU states. These 'could lead to increased competition from countries with lower food standards, animal welfare standards and environmental protection. This risks putting UK farmers at a competitive disadvantage,' the Environmental Audit Committee warned. The agricultural sector also relies heavily on seasonal migrant labour from the Continent (see Immigration chapter). Mary Creagh, the committee chair, said:

> Changes from Brexit could put our countryside, farming and wildlife at risk. UK farming faces significant risks – from a loss of subsidies and tariffs on farm exports, to increased competition from countries with weaker food, animal welfare and environmental standards. The government must not trade away these key protections as we leave the EU.

Meurig Raymond, president of the NFU, told the Oxford Farming Conference that tariff-free access to the single market 'has got to be the top priority ... the number two priority is access to competent labour for seasonal and permanent work on farms'.

Some analysts argue that the CAP has maintained farming practices which long ago became unviable, such as sheep rearing, and the new British agricultural policy should take more radical steps. For George Monbiot, the almost-vegan environmental activist, the subsidy system 'sustains the greatest cause of habitat and wildlife destruction in Britain'. He added:

> Sheep have not so much altered the ecosystem as removed it altogether, stripping most edible plants and much of the soil from the land, leaving nothing of what would once have been a rich mosaic of forest and glade except coarse grass, occasionally interspersed with bracken and bare rock: the only things the sheep can't eat … The area that is grazed by sheep in Britain is broadly equivalent to our entire arable acreage. In other words, this is an astonishingly profligate use of land. It is hard to think of any industry, anywhere on earth, with a higher ratio of destruction to production. Because it is uneconomic, it depends entirely on European money. It should be a source of enduring shame to Britain's big conservation groups that, out of sheer cowardice, they refuse to confront this pointless mass erasure of wildlife at public expense … As soon as the money appears on national accounts, it will become politically unsustainable.

Monbiot's proposed solution was for a future rural subsidy system that paid 'only for the delivery of public goods – such as restoring ecosystems, preventing flooding downstream, and bringing children and adults back into contact with the living world'. Measures would also be needed to curtail the power of supermarkets to end the 'outrageous' situation that farmers receive only 9 per cent of the value of their produce sold by them.

The post-Brexit government may be tempted by an even more radical example of reform for the farm sector, especially if there is a squeeze on public sector spending. In New Zealand, faced with an economic crisis of high inflation, rising unemployment, soaring government debt and state agricultural funding amounting to 4 per cent of GDP, the Labour government of David Lange decided in 1984 on a dramatic phase-out of all farm subsidies. The impact was huge – farmers took to the streets in protest, many went out of business and most had to rethink their business model and introduce new methods and products. By 2005, twenty years after the reforms, there were one-third fewer sheep and beef meat farms. Venison production grew from nothing to 2 million deer worth US$100 million a year in exports.[82] By 2015, the sheep flock reduced from 70 million before the reforms to 29 million but lambing rates increased by a quarter, as did carcass weights. Dairy cattle increased from 2.3 million to 6.5 million.[83] There was a massive shift away from meat production to horticulture and wine. Kiwi fruit exports rose from NZ$172 million in 1985 to NZ$1.2 billion in 2015, while wine exports grew from NZ$3 million to NZ$1.4 billion over the same period.[84] Overall employment on farms did not change much because although meat, dairy and arable farms got bigger and more efficient, there was a growth in smaller and more labour-intensive horticultural production.

Roger Douglas, New Zealand's Minister of Finance from 1984 to 1988, who oversaw the reforms, said he thought Britain could benefit from the New Zealand experience. 'I am sure it could translate,' he said.

We went from a level of subsidies estimated at around 30 per cent to virtually nothing in a relatively short period of time and what it demonstrated was how people can adapt. And if you talk to New Zealand farmers now, you would not find them wanting to go back to where they were. When you take the subsidies, what happens is that land that has been brought into a form of production based on the subsidies; that form of production on that particular land is no longer viable so people begin to do something else with the land. They get smart about it – it might be just planting trees but they might look at other forms of production. When you have subsidies, people will be grazing sheep or cattle or doing something with that land for which it was not really suited. If you lower subsidies you will see a great deal more innovation.[85]

Jim Sutton, New Zealand's Agriculture Minister in 1990 and again from 1999 to 2005, said that farmers were 'stunned' by the end of agricultural subsidies announced in the 1984 budget, leading to 'huge protest marches' across the country.

As a new back-bench MP, myself a farmer, I was exposed

to the full fury. The farmers were driven by fear. Many believed they could not survive in this new circumstance. Deregulated interest rates for farm finance soared. Fast forward three years to the next general election. Far fewer farm businesses than expected had failed. It had been tough but the reforms were working. Government initiatives to write off a proportion of state-held farm debt to the most stressed farmers had helped. Farmers were proud of their newly rediscovered resilience. They were rapidly coming to the view that the whole reform had been their idea in the first place. Has the UK the political stomach to follow a similar path? I cannot answer that, but as the sobering realities of the post-Brexit economy set in, it may be possible. It has worked for us, and we are mostly of British stock.[86]

This type of reform would be hugely controversial and disruptive. A Dutch study in 2010 found that 15 per cent of UK farms would be unviable under a totally liberalised system similar to the New Zealand removal of subsidies.[87] The Open Europe think tank commented:

As is often the case with liberalisation, the outcome could be greater specialisation. Types of farming better able to compete will be boosted and draw in capital and labour, while those that are not will fall by the wayside. This of course could have a serious impact on employment and see a number of firms going out of business … Employment in agriculture is not evenly distributed around the UK – in 2014 it accounted for 1.1% of total employment in England, compared to 2.5% in Scotland, 4.2% in Wales, and 5.8% in Northern Ireland. Significant job losses from farms unable to function under a liberalised regime would therefore have wider social implications for the regions most affected. The flipside to such disruption would likely be lower prices. If tariffs were removed, the consumer support of between £400m and £1.4bn for UK farmers would no longer exist and this could be realised, at least partially, by consumers. Furthermore, the greater competition and specialisation could drive prices even lower.[88]

The EU bans certain farm practices which are widely used in nations with whom Britain wants to forge new trade agreements. The US will be keen to export its beef reared with growth-enhancing hormones and chicken washed in chlorinated water, both of which are barred from entering the EU over health fears.

Bob Young of the American Farm Bureau Federation, the largest farm organisation in the US, said:

It is a question of science and I think we have shown it is a safe product … [Brexit] is an opportunity for us to get products which have been demonstrated to be extremely safe, which we have been consuming here in the United States for decades, to be able to have science-based decisions on whether products are allowed into a country or not – that would be very strong on our agenda.[89]

In response, Martin Howarth, director of strategy at the NFU, said it would be 'completely unreasonable' for a trade deal to allow entry into Britain of products farmed with techniques that were not allowed in the UK. Asked if he would like British farmers to be able to use the US practices for beef and chicken, he added:

I think it would depend on what consumers would accept … it is a question of science and we would like to follow the science. The science is probably clear on both of the issues … There has got to be equality of treatment here and what would be unacceptable is that we are importing product using methods that we are not able to use here.

There are clearly many decisions to be made about the post-2020 future for farming, from the radical New Zealand approach of scrapping all government funding right through to the highly supportive model still favoured across Europe, including in non-EU nations Norway and Switzerland, where huge sums are spent combined with high import duty barriers. Norway provides its farmers with 60 per cent of their average income, according to the OECD. The devolved administrations of the UK are responsible for administering Common Agricultural Policy payments and would expect to be in control of farm funding after Brexit, which will see different approaches develop in England, Scotland, Wales and Northern Ireland. Meanwhile the EU system of direct subsidies based on the size of farms, uncapped by the British government, has provided an unexpected Brexit bonus for some of the largest and wealthiest landowners in the UK. The official exchange rate for EU payments was set at 85p to the euro for 2016 compared with 73p the previous year following the dramatic fall in the pound after the referendum decision on 23 June.[90] That meant an extra handout to the Queen's farms at Sandringham and Windsor of about £150,000 on top of the £965,000 received in 2015 and an increase of £65,000 for the stud farms of Prince Khalid Abdullah Al Saud.

CHAPTER 6

FISHING

The historic town of Whitby on England's north-east coast is famous for its fish and chips. The Magpie Café was praised by chef Rick Stein as the one which 'opened my eyes to how good a chip shop could be', Mister Chips was called 'beyond belief brilliant' by Jeremy Clarkson, while Quayside won the national Fish & Chip Awards in 2014. A century ago, 180 fishing boats operated out of the port, supplying the local restaurants and many more beyond with fresh cod and haddock. By the 1980s, the number of trawlers was down to two dozen. Today, the historic harbour is quiet save for the crab fishers and inshore angling boats that take tourists out for the day. Fishing families who have lived through the decline reserve much of the blame for the European Union. After forty years at sea, fisherman Howard Locker sold his whitefish trawler *Whitby Rose* in 2014 because the running costs were too high and, along with his son Craig, joined those staying close to shore catching crabs and shellfish. The restrictions in EU waters from Brussels, with quotas and limits on days at sea which hamstrung the trawler, do not apply within the national twelve-mile coastal fishing zone. 'First I went to sea with one hand behind my back. Then it was both hands. The EU has been a disaster for fishing,' Locker said.[91] That left just one family-owned trawler based at the Yorkshire port. A few other larger vessels are registered here but operate out of Scotland, often fishing in Norwegian waters and landing their catch in Peterhead in Aberdeenshire or in Denmark. Most of the town's famous fish and chip restaurants get their fresh supplies mainly from Peterhead, the UK's largest landing port for fish, and often use Icelandic cod and Norwegian haddock. The Scarborough region which includes Whitby voted by 62 per cent to 38 per cent in the referendum to leave the EU and it was a similar story in many traditional fishing communities, with Kingston upon Hull voting by 67.6 to 32.4 for Brexit and North East Lincolnshire, which includes Grimsby, by 69.9 to 30.1. A survey just before the EU referendum found that 92 per cent of fishermen would vote to leave – 'a uniformity of opinion that is unmatched by any other economic or social group in the UK'.[92]

Few industries have been so grotesquely mismanaged as fishing under the EU's Common Fisheries Policy (CFP). Under annual quotas decided in Brussels every December by politicians who routinely disregarded scientific advice, 48 per cent of Atlantic stocks and 93 per cent of Mediterranean stocks were classified as over-fished in 2015. The EU spent €2.73 billion between 1994 and 2013 in compensation to owners to scrap vessels, but over-capacity still increased by 3 per cent a year.[93] One million tonnes of dead or dying fish were thrown back every year by fishermen given tight quotas of what they could bring back to harbour, until a long over-due reform of the CFP agreed in 2013 set out a new system allowing all fish caught to be landed by phasing in a discard ban between 2015 and 2019.

The original CFP was hastily planned by the founding six EEC members ahead of the accession of the seafaring nations of Britain, Ireland and Denmark in 1973. It came into force in 1976.[94] Until this point, the 'freedom of the seas' meant that British fishermen were able to chase fish stocks which lay beyond the territorial waters claimed by coastal nations, which at this point did not usually extend by more than twelve nautical miles from the shore. The quantity of fish landed in the UK peaked at 1.2 million tonnes in 1913, varied between 0.9 and 1.1 million tonnes in the interwar period, and hit a modern peak of 1.0 million tonnes in 1973, the year Britain joined the European club. Landings went into steady decline, stabilising at around 0.4 million tonnes a year since 2009.[95] While shellfish catches have risen by 15 per cent between 1995 and 2015, up to 149,000 tonnes, reflecting the decision of many fishermen to switch to domestic-controlled coastal waters like the Lockers of Whitby, the main decline in landings since 1998 has been in demersal fish – those which live near the bottom of the sea – falling by 63 per cent from 457,000 tonnes in 1998 to 168,000 tonnes in 2015. Within this group of fish, catches of whiting, haddock and cod have declined the most.[96] The number of fishermen has fallen from just under 50,000 in 1938 to 12,107 in 2015. At the end of 2015, the number of vessels registered in the UK fleet stood at 6,187, almost 30 per cent down on 1996.[97]

The EU was not solely to blame for the dramatic decline in the UK fishing industry. Britain's entry into the European club coincided with the 'cod wars' with Iceland over fishing rights in the North Atlantic at a time when technology and state subsidies to buy vessels were making it possible to catch more and more in unregulated waters. Iceland's declaration of a 200-mile exclusive fishing zone, which brought the conflict to an end in 1976, spelled the end of Britain's distant-water fleet. It led the third United Nations Conference on the Law of the Sea to set the general rule that any sovereign coastal nation has a right to an Exclusive Economic Zone (EEZ) of 200 nautical miles, putting not only Icelandic waters but also Greenland, the Faroes and Norway off limits to British trawlers apart from where historical or reciprocal access could be negotiated. Meanwhile the UK's EEZ, apart from its coastal national waters, became a shared resource with its European partners.

'In the 1970s, you were moving from a situation where outside territorial limits it was a free-for-all,' said Barrie Deas, chief executive of the National Federation of Fishermen's Organisations (NFFO).

If you look at landings in the 1950s and 1960s, the bulk of them in terms of tonnage of white fish were coming from Icelandic and Norwegian waters. Then the international law of the sea changed and that had very profound implications for the British fishing industry. The 200-mile exclusive zone became the international norm and this as well as the need for sound management of shared stocks coincided with the UK's entry to the EU. The consequence was more or less the collapse of the British distant-water fleet, which was the backbone of the fishing industry. The trawling industry based in Hull, Grimsby, Milford Haven, Fleetwood, Aberdeen – the big company fleets that went up to Iceland in big ships fishing for white fish – it more or less disappeared. Grimsby had 400 vessels; now they do not have any. The distant-water fleet now is three or four or five vessels depending on the year. This had nothing to do with the EU, but you then had the existing members of the Common Market, faced with the UK's application for entry, slamming in a condition which was the principle of equal access to a common resource.[98]

British waters account for 13 per cent of the EU's Exclusive Economic Zone. Other EU nations were also able to fish within six miles of the twelve-mile national coastal zone due to historic rights of access. Research by the North Atlantic Fisheries College Marine Centre in Shetland in October 2016 showed that 58 per cent of the fish and shellfish landed from the UK's EEZ by EU fishing boats was caught by non-UK boats during 2012 to 2014.[99] This study showed that vessels from the rest of the EU landed 650,000 tonnes of fish and shellfish from the UK's EEZ each year, worth £408 million. This included 99,000 tonnes (£179 million) of demersal fish, 424,000 tonnes (£183 million) of pelagic (non-coastal) fish, 16,000 tonnes (£34 million) of shellfish, and 111,000 tonnes (£11 million) of industrial fish. In contrast, UK fishing boats landed 90,000 tonnes of fish and shellfish, worth £103 million, from other areas of the EU's EEZ each year – just one quarter of the value taken by EU vessels in Britain's 200-mile waters. In other words, non-UK European fishing boats landed 560,000 tonnes (worth £300 million) more fish and shellfish from Britain's EEZ each year than UK fishing boats landed from elsewhere in the European Union's EEZ, showing the dramatic one-sidedness of the EU principle of shared access to a common resource. This meant that non-UK European fishing boats landed seven times more fish and shellfish by weight from British waters than UK boats did from other areas of the EU's EEZ and four times more by value. Half of the demersal fish, almost two-thirds of the pelagic fish and almost all of the industrial fish landed from Britain's EEZ were caught by non-UK boats from the EU, including more than half of the plaice, three-quarters of the Dover sole, hake, skate, rays and herring, 83 per cent of the horse mackerel and 94 per cent of the blue whiting.

The Common Fisheries Policy at first encouraged

over-fishing, through generous subsidies to build more boats, and then under its quota system from 1983 attempted to rein in fishermen with increasingly drastic restrictions.[100] The quota system was based on catch statistics from the previous five years which, in one of its most absurdly one-sided allocations, gives France 84 per cent of Channel cod compared to 9 per cent for the UK. Many boats fished 'mixed' waters, so endangered fish were often hauled in along with more plentiful varieties. A tight quota for cod meant it was illegal to land any cod caught above the allocation and they had to be thrown back. This led to the increasingly crazy situation of one mature cod being thrown back, dead, for every one landed. All in the name of conserving the species. In another piece of classic CFP poor management, the EU decided that smaller boats should not be closely regulated, leaving vessels of under ten metres to fish more or less freely within general catch limits. That led to skippers getting rid of larger vessels – often with EU compensation – and building a new generation of very wide boats just under the ten-metre limit. These 'small' vessels could out-fish many much larger ones. And so the fish allocation for the under-ten-metre class was no longer enough to keep everyone in business.

Spain had the largest fishing fleet in Europe and with the country's accession to the EEC in 1986, the British government wanted to preserve a strong national fishing fleet in UK waters that was, as far as possible, British-owned and crewed, and based in UK ports. Under a pre-membership agreement in 1980, Spanish companies had already been re-registering in the UK using legislation from 1894 that allowed fishing rights to any vessel owned by a British subject or incorporated in the UK and having its main business there. Upon joining the European club, Spanish companies began buying up British vessels together with their licences so they were able to fish anywhere in EEC waters, land their fish in Spain and count their catch as British quota. The Merchant Shipping Act 1988 imposed a new condition that British-registered fishing vessels must be at least 75 per cent owned by British citizens, or by companies where at least 75 per cent of shares were in the hands of British citizens. This had the effect of suspending fishing by the 'Anglo-Spanish' vessels sailing under the British flag and became the subject of a bitter court battle which ended up at the CJEU. In 1991, the European judges found that the Merchant Shipping Act was in breach of the freedom of establishment rules set out in the EEC treaty. This stated that nationals from any member nation had 'the right to take up and pursue activities as self-employed persons' in any other member nation 'under the conditions laid down for its own nationals by the law of the country where such establishment is effected'.[101] The case, known as Factortame after the main Spanish company, became a landmark in EU law because it was the first time an existing British national law had been struck down by the CJEU for being incompatible with the European treaties. The Spanish vessels not only won access to British waters; the ruling confirmed their right to buy up

British fishing quotas, providing the boats were managed from within the UK. In March 2000, Factortame and almost ninety other Anglo-Spanish fishing companies accepted an offer of compensation from the British government of £55 million.

The Brexit vote came, ironically, just as the EU's much-maligned Common Fisheries Policy was beginning to see benefits from radical reforms in 2013 pushed hard by the British government. These returned a lot of decision-making powers to national authorities and took measures to end the scandal of discards. Cod stocks have been steadily growing for a decade. Outside of the EU, the fishing nation which decided in a referendum not to join the European club in 1973 has been able to manage its fisheries in a very different way over the past four decades. The traditional way of life for coastal communities in Norway has been preserved because its fishing industry is not subject to EU law under the terms of the country's relationship with Brussels. Unlike trawler men elsewhere in Europe, Norwegian fishermen do not have to share their waters with foreign rivals unless they swap quotas in annual discussions each autumn with the EU. Numerous fishing villages owe their existence to laws designed to maintain the rural population and small family fishing companies. Inge Halstensen, who represented Norway in fishing negotiations for almost thirty years, said:

We have legislation making it impossible to build big

companies in fishing. The fishing boat industry is frag-
mented, based on small units, very often one company,
one boat … It has been Norwegian policy to use the fishing
industry to employ and settle all the coast – and we have
a long coast. A company from Britain cannot come here
or to Iceland, the same with the Faroe Islands. This rule
forbidding foreigners, you find it in all of the countries
outside the EU. It seemed that Brussels did not understand
that way of thinking.[102]

Mr Halstensen watched as Brussels represented Britain and
the other member states in international talks. Norway would
give some of its cod to the EU and it was often given mackerel
and blue whiting in British waters in return. 'As far as I can
see the British are paying and Spain, Germany, Netherlands
get access to the north sector and fish there. We also fish blue
whiting in Irish waters. Why? Because Spain, Germany, Netherlands are fishing haddock in Norwegian waters.'

There is little prospect of Britain imitating Norway's heavily
subsidised model, with its prohibition on foreign ownership
and on companies growing bigger than three or four vessels.
Brexit will, however, mean Britain will have much more say
over who fishes in its territorial waters and will want to right
some obvious wrongs, such as the French claiming 84 per
cent of Channel cod in a zone where national waters are divided roughly 50/50 between the two countries. Renegotiating
quota shares is one of the top aims of the UK fishing industry.

Norway's tough defence of its territorial waters in international fishing talks will be a model, according to Barry Deas.

We recognise where you have shared stocks – and more than 100 of our stocks are shared with the member states simply because of geography and biology – then you need shared management. But in the future it will not be the December Council of Ministers in Brussels that decides for us, it will be international negotiations. It is not dissimilar to what the EU already does with Norway: they sit down each autumn and agree on the joint stocks. The North Sea has the most important ones – cod, haddock, whiting, plaice – all of those are agreed in the context of annual reciprocal fisheries agreement between the EU and Norway. So the most likely model for agreeing harvest rates for shared stocks is bilateral or trilateral agreements on the international stage that will cover that total amount to be harvested each year for each stock. That is where we expect the UK's quota shares to move towards more closely reflecting the stocks that are in our waters. We may wish to trade some of that off for fishing opportunities elsewhere but that's a decision for us to make in the context of the negotiations.

There is no forum for settling international fishing disputes, however, and the possibility remains of protracted 'fish wars' returning if the UK wants to regain quota aggressively. Complicating the attempt to exclude foreign boats from British waters will be possible retaliatory measures led by countries which buy UK fish. France, Spain and Ireland bought over 140,000 tonnes of UK fish in 2014/15 and account for 36 per cent of the total amount exported to the UK's top twenty export markets.[103]

'The EU, for all its faults, did have a framework for making timely decisions and a dispute resolution arrangement, ultimately the European Court of Justice [CJEU], and it is a worry, it is a thought, how do you stop disputes escalating?' said Deas.

> How do you come to timely decisions – and the first of those would be putting a cap on the total amount taken out. Countries can set autonomous quotas but this is a second best because there is always the danger that everybody takes a little bit extra and before long the scientists are saying the trend in fishing mortality is going up again. The UN Convention on the Law of the Sea lays down principles that countries should cooperate to ensure rational harvesting but I am not aware of any dispute mechanism. With the [recent] mackerel dispute between Faroes, Iceland, Norway and the EU, after two or three years of jostling for position, the countries more or less agreed but there was no legal structure there to force them.

Britain should not hesitate about claiming back full control over its EEZ waters, even if the EU slaps import tariffs on

British fish, according to Bertie Armstrong, chief executive of the Scottish Fisherman's Federation. 'More than half of our natural resource goes elsewhere. That is unthinkable for another coastal state. Taking that back is not an act of regression, it is an act of normality ... This is a natural resource which belongs to us – and the law is on our side,' he said.[104] He said the World Trade Organization tariff on fish was 5 to 10 per cent and the UK should not be 'frightened to death' by any trade tariffs that could be introduced following Brexit.

> We are not going to be in the single market. We do not need the single market. We need an adequate market to press our product abroad ... Some small tariffs would not necessarily be a disaster, particularly as the other side of the coin is that you may access new markets like India.

The European Parliament will fight to safeguard EU access to UK waters and the ability to register under the British flag, according to a leaked memo from its fisheries committee in February 2017. It drafted seven provisions it wanted to see in Britain's exit agreement, including the stipulation that there would be 'no increase to the UK's share of fishing opportunities for jointly fished stocks [maintaining the existing quota distribution in UK and EU waters]'.[105] The document added that in order for the UK and EU to keep to commitments on sustainable fishing, 'it is difficult to see any alternative to the continued application of the common fisheries policy'.

As well as 'reciprocal access for the EU and UK fleets to the fishing grounds in the UK and the EU waters', measures must be included in any exit deal 'ensuring the maintenance of the same legal conditions for UK-registered vehicles, without requiring stronger economic links that could virtually make it impossible for EU vessel-owners managing UK flagged vessels to continue operating in the UK'.

It remains an open question whether Brexit will see the revival of fishing activity at towns all along the eastern English coast, which were hardest-hit by the Common Fisheries Policy. Adrian Fusco, whose family owns three restaurants in Whitby, dreams of returning to local fish at Quayside, his flagship restaurant opposite the fish quay. 'I would love to serve fish landed in Whitby, just across the street,' he said.[106]

CHAPTER 7

FLYING

Stelios Haji-Ioannou was just twenty-eight when he founded Britain's first modern low-cost airline, aiming to make flying 'as affordable as a pair of jeans'. EasyJet launched its service on the Luton to Glasgow route but the real goal was always to pioneer a new era of cheap travel to the Continent. The path had already been prepared by Ryanair, based in Dublin, the first low-cost airline to make use of the European single market 'double disapproval' regime between member nations. It meant that authorities in both the country of take-off and the country of landing had to object to prevent a new operator entering the market. This enabled Ryanair to begin flying from Dublin to the UK despite resistance from the Irish government, after Margaret Thatcher's government gave it the green light. It was the first step towards breaking the monopoly of the national flag-carrier airlines which kept ticket prices high – Ryanair halved the price of flying from Dublin to London overnight. The next big breakthrough was made by EasyJet when it established the first low-cost route from Britain to continental Europe in 1996. Again, there was resistance. This time it came from Schiphol airport in Amsterdam, the initial mainland Europe destination, in the form of a fax to EasyJet head office shortly before the inaugural flight. 'I strongly advise you to reconsider your current plan and maybe look into more profitable European destinations. We would not like to see one of Europe's pioneering low-fare carriers go under because of a highly competitive and unprofitable Amsterdam operation,' it said. Schiphol said it already had fifty flights a day to London, many at competitive prices, and that EasyJet's aircraft were too noisy. EasyJet said its sound levels were within legal limits and it was in the process of buying quieter planes. Haji-Ioannou refused to be put off. He added Nice and Barcelona to EasyJet's EU destinations two months later and the airline never looked back. By 2016, EasyJet was flying forty routes from Amsterdam and had become the second-largest carrier from Schiphol after the Dutch airline KLM. It was Britain's biggest airline by passenger volume, carrying 74.5 million in 2016 on 874 routes in and between more than thirty countries. Haji-Ioannou received a knighthood in 2006 for services to entrepreneurship but quit the EasyJet board in 2010 in a dispute over expansion plans while remaining the largest shareholder. In 2014, the company told a government review: 'EasyJet is a product of the EU's deregulation of Europe's aviation market. Without deregulation we would not exist.'[107]

Until the single market became a reality in 1986, upstart new airlines had come and gone in Europe as the government-owned flag-carriers squeezed them out. The most heroic failure of all was Laker Airways, founded by British entrepreneur Sir Freddie Laker and based at Gatwick until it was eventually bullied out of business in 1982 by British Airways and the government's preferred second provider, British Caledonian, itself later bought up by BA. Laker found it hard to win flight slots, which were negotiated on a bilateral basis with other countries by the government, with preference given to the state-owned flag-carrier.

Across the other side of the Atlantic, the 1978 Airline Deregulation Act completely liberalised the US market and showed Europe the way. Over here, meanwhile, it was a decade-long process in the wake of the Single European Act of 1986. Successive sets of EU measures gradually opened up jealously protected national aviation fiefdoms and it became the first mode of transport – and effectively still the only one – to benefit from a fully integrated competitive single market. The first and second legislative packages of 1987 and 1990 started to relax the rules governing fares and capacities. In 1992, the third package removed all remaining commercial restrictions for European airlines operating within the EU, setting up the European Single Aviation Market. This was extended to Norway and Iceland and the opportunity was grabbed by Norwegian Air Shuttle, now Europe's third-biggest budget airline behind Ryanair and EasyJet. The third package substituted 'Community air carriers' for national air carriers and set the basic principle that any European Community air carrier could set fares for passengers and cargo, and access any intra-EU route, without any permit or authorisation required beyond its national air operator certificate (AOC). Community air carriers have to be owned and effectively controlled by nationals of member nations and their principal place of business located in a member nation. Regulations from 1993 stated that congested airport flight slots should be allocated to airlines in an equitable and transparent manner by an independent 'slot coordinator'.[108] A directive in 1996 opened up the market for ground-handling services, and a directive in 2009 set the basic principles for airport charges paid by carriers for the use of facilities and services.[109] National safety rules for passengers and aircraft were replaced by common safety rules and a European Aviation Safety Agency (EASA) was set up in Cologne in 2003 to prepare the rules, set technical standards and certify staff. The four countries in the European Free Trade Association (EFTA) also take part in EASA and have non-voting seats on the board.

Low-cost airlines enabled by the EU have transformed travel for millions of Britons. In 1973, UK airlines flew 17.4 million passengers and UK airports handled 43.1 million passengers.[110] In 2015, UK airlines flew 128.9 million passengers and UK airports handled 233.6 million passengers.[111] The low-cost carriers brought a wider choice of destinations and lower fares, especially where two of the budget airlines competed on the route. One study of the route from London to Toulouse in southern France showed how British Airways and Air France were charging £910 for a return ticket, or £246 provided there was a Saturday night stay, before Ryanair entered the market in 2002. The Irish airline charged £187 for return flights to Carcassonne, 100km to the south-east of Toulouse, forcing a reduction in BA's price to £273, or £198 with a Saturday night, and similar cuts by Air France. When EasyJet joined in three years after Ryanair, offering £91 return flights from Gatwick to Toulouse, BA charged £193 and Ryanair £112. Air France pulled out of the route.[112] From 1995 to 2014, passenger miles travelled on all modes of transport within the EU increased by around 23 per cent, while for flying the figure jumped by 74 per cent. Aviation's share of total passenger transport increased from 6.5 per cent to 9.2 per cent – by far the strongest growth in all modes of transport.[113]

In 2006, the European Single Aviation Market was extended to include eight south-east European countries (three of which – Bulgaria, Romania and Croatia – have since become EU members) to form the European Common Aviation Area (ECAA). This gave airlines based in thirty-six nations, including Albania and Serbia, the right to fly on routes between any airport within the ECAA area provided the countries accept all EU laws on aviation plus the jurisdiction of the CJEU. Membership of the ECAA has to be ratified by every existing member nation. The non-EU members of the ECAA have all decided that the advantages of being within a fully integrated aviation market with a shared rulebook and common dispute settlement mechanism are worth the downside of not being able to take part in making or amending the laws governing it.

Brussels is not only responsible for commercial aviation within the Continent but also makes agreements on behalf of all member nations on flying rights to non-EU countries and has made numerous deals, including with the US, Canada, Norway and Israel. Before joining the EEC, Britain negotiated bilateral aviation agreements with individual countries, such as the Bermuda Agreement with the US, originally signed in 1946 and named after the island where the negotiations took place. Updated in 1977 and again in 1995, the agreement was challenged by the European Commission because it allowed the US to block EU airlines from valuable transatlantic flying slots based if they were not British 'owned and controlled', and even though the UK government allowed other EU airlines to use Heathrow. Judges at the CJEU ruled in 2002 that the UK's bilateral agreement with the US was in breach of the EU treaty guarantee on freedom of establishment.[114] This guarantee stated that:

Restrictions on the freedom of establishment of nationals of a Member State in the territory of another Member State shall be prohibited ... Freedom of establishment shall include the right to ... manage undertakings, in particular companies or firms ... under the conditions laid down for its own nationals by the law of the country where such establishment is effected.[115]

The CJEU made further judgments annulling bilateral agreements between seven other member countries and the US and then Brussels set about negotiating the EU–US Open Skies Agreement, which has overseen transatlantic flying from 2008, effectively making it easier for other EU airlines to fly on the most sought-after route from Heathrow to JFK in New York. After Brexit, the UK will need to revert to a bilateral deal with the US and all other destinations – talks which may take some time given the volume of agreements to be settled.

Theresa May's declarations in her Lancaster House speech in January 2017 that 'we do not seek membership of the single market' and 'we will take back control of our laws and bring an end to the jurisdiction of the European Court of Justice [CJEU] in Britain' threw the UK aviation industry into uncertainty. May added that 'instead we seek the greatest possible access to [the single market] through a new, comprehensive, bold and ambitious free trade agreement'. According to the International Air Transport Association (IATA), 'the EU is easily the single biggest destination market from the UK, accounting for 49 per cent of passengers and 54 per cent of scheduled commercial flights'.[116] May's declaration meant that Britain could not be part of the European Single Aviation Market and by extension the ECAA unless all members agreed to give it special dispensation not to be covered by the

CJEU. Negotiating either access to the ECAA or a new bilateral relationship with it will be one of the first tests of that strategy, given the many months' notice that airlines need to organise their route planning. IATA said that:

> in effect the choice comes down to a trade-off between two key issues; access for UK airlines and customers to the European Single Aviation Market and policy freedom for the UK to set its own regulations … In addition to market access, the UK participates in numerous technical programs to facilitate the movement of both passengers and cargo. Continued participation in these schemes will also have an impact on UK competitiveness.[117]

EasyJet could find itself a victim of its own success during the talks to reset Britain's aviation agreement with the EU. Some European airlines are thought likely to put pressure on their governments to restrict access and reduce the competition they face from the British low-cost airline. EasyJet has its air operating certificate (AOC) in Britain and one in Switzerland (which is outside the ECAA) to enable it to fly planes there. Given the possibility for such turbulence, in 2016 EasyJet decided to apply for a new AOC in another EU member nation. While it would keep its main base in Britain, a new European AOC would enable it to remain within the EU system and protect the 30 per cent of its network that operates wholly between or within continental countries, providing it can satisfy EU ownership requirements. This plan came at a price. EasyJet reportedly needed to spend £10 million to cover establishing the AOC and the re-registration of aircraft.

Similarly, Ryanair might have to apply for a UK AOC if the UK exits the EU without a reciprocal deal on cabotage – the right to fly between airports in one aviation zone – because its Irish AOC would still cover all flights involving ECAA airports but not its routes from one British airport to another within Britain. Ryanair suggested in February 2017 that the lack of a clear post-Brexit deal could see the company cutting UK services. Kenny Jacobs, the airline's chief marketing officer, said it needed to know the new relationship between Britain and the ECAA quickly to help planning. 'If we don't know this time next year, what are airlines going to do? Are we going to have to make significant capacity cuts?'[118] If the UK was to seek an 'open skies' deal with the ECAA, it would require the assent of all members, with the possibility that individual grievances could hold up agreement.

And here is where Britain could come up against a 300-year-old problem that could complicate aviation talks. Spain opposes any legal agreements implying that Gibraltar's airport is under British control. Madrid argues that Gibraltar airport is illegally situated on Spanish land that was not included in the 1713 Treaty of Utrecht that handed some territory to Britain. One Spanish diplomat said: 'Any EU agreement with the UK on aviation cannot apply to the airport of Gibraltar. A deal that is applicable to the airport of Gibraltar would imply recognition of the legal right of the UK to the territory.'[119] Four airlines use Gibraltar airport, with up to nine arrivals a day from the UK or Morocco – British Airways, EasyJet, Monarch and Royal Air Maroc. It has symbolic importance way beyond its low level of activity. Several EU aviation law changes have been held up by the dispute for years. Philip Hammond, when Foreign Secretary, accused the Spanish government in 2014 of using the issue as a way of 'forcing sovereignty negotiations on Gibraltar'. The Rock could become a stumbling block to aviation after Brexit.

The first and most obvious way that Brexit affected airline passengers was in the dramatic fall in the value of the pound after the vote. EasyJet posted a 27.9 per cent drop in pre-tax profits to £495 million for the year to September 2016 after the sharply weaker pound cost it £88 million. In January 2017, it forecast a full-year hit of £105 million from the weaker pound because fuel costs were priced in dollars. Willie Walsh, chief executive of International Airlines Group (IAG), which owns British Airways, Vueling, Aer Lingus and Iberia, said that fares would be flat in 2017 after two years of falling prices. IAG reported pre-tax profits up by a third to €2.4 billion in 2016 but said a slump in the value of the pound since the EU referendum cost the company €460 million.[120] 'More than a quarter of revenues for Ryanair come from the UK,' said John Strickland, an independent aviation consultant.

Even if the UK remains fairly strong in terms of demand,

by the time they have remitted their sterling earnings into euros they have earned less even though the ticket price remains the same. They could think they could find something more profitable for their aircraft to do without worrying about the exchange rate. They could take them out of the UK so there is a risk of routes being lost. Then there is the issue of spending money to get a licence – is it worth Ryanair bothering to get an UK AOC when they only do a few domestic routes in the UK? They could stop them. Short-term consumers may not see a difference but I think there are some genuine risks as people in the UK begin to realise their spending power for a beach holiday in Spain, or to the US, is reduced. Airlines might pull schedules if they see demand changing.[121]

Passengers have won extensive rights to assistance such as meals and hotel accommodation as well as compensation for flight delays and refunds for cancellations through an EU regulation which came into force in 2005.[122] Its effectiveness has been boosted by court judgments in the UK and at the CJEU. Passengers are entitled to refreshments and 'communication' if the expected delay is more than two hours for a short-haul flight, three hours for a medium-distance flight and four hours for long-haul. If the delayed flight is expected to depart on the next day, passengers are entitled to accommodation. If a flight is delayed by five hours, passengers can abandon their journey and receive a refund for all unused tickets, a refund on tickets used already if the flight no longer serves any purpose and a flight back to their original point of departure. Court decisions have established that a passenger delayed by three hours or more is entitled to compensation as though their flight had been cancelled. Cash compensation is a payment of €250 for short-haul, €400 for medium and €600 for long-haul. Airlines are not obliged to pay compensation under the regulation in the case of 'extraordinary circumstances', a term which has been subject to much legal wrangling. The CJEU ruled technical faults were not extraordinary circumstances. In a case against Ryanair, the CJEU ruled in 2013 that natural disasters such as the eruption of the Icelandic volcano Eyjafjallajökull and its volcanic ash cloud which shut down most European air traffic, qualified as 'extraordinary circumstances', so no compensation was payable for delays or cancellations. However, it said the airlines still had an obligation to provide care such as meals and refreshments for stranded passengers, including a hotel room and transportation to the hotel if an overnight stay was necessary.[123] Ryanair said the ruling 'will materially increase the cost of flying across Europe and consumer airfares will increase as airlines will be obliged to recover the cost of these claims from their customers'.

A whole sub-industry has grown up of companies offering to help passengers claim compensation under the EU rules. Airlines have been accused of trying to dodge payments running into millions of pounds. In turn, the airlines have attacked the claims companies as 'ambulance-chasers'. Michael

O'Leary, chief executive of Ryanair, was asked about the EU compensation payments in an earnings call in February 2017 and forecast they would rise:

> The ambulance chasers, the claims management companies, particularly in the UK ... are again engaged in thoroughly disreputable practices. They're trying to get customers to sign up unbeknowingly and then deducting up to 50 per cent of the €261 money from the customer, whereas what we're trying to do is get the customer to write directly to us. Really it's a much simpler process now because the courts have, over time, determined what extraordinary circumstances are, whether they're paid whether the claim period is two years or six years. So now we're processing a lot more of them because we're querying a lot less issues. It becomes a ridiculous amount of money, particularly when your average fare is now €33 and a customer for a three-hour delay can claim up to €250 in compensation, more than six times the average fare paid ... It's an issue that we deal with. And, remember, we're not responsible for the weather but we are responsible for right-to-care costs during adverse weather situations.[124]

As with all EU regulations, Britain will co-opt the EU compensation regime under the Great Repeal Bill. It will only be free to amend or repeal the legislation if it leaves the ECAA, because enforcement of EU compensation and passenger care standards are mandatory for members. If Britain does not join the ECAA, the regulation could be repealed but the UK is likely to bring in its own scheme, so savings for airlines – and therefore passengers – could be minimal.

CHAPTER 8

IMMIGRATION

Jack Straw made a fateful announcement in December 2002 which helped set Britain on the road to Brexit. The Labour government had decided 'to extend to citizens of the new EU member states, from their accession on 1 May 2004, the full rights to work in the UK as enjoyed by existing EU citizens.'[125] It was up to each of the fifteen 'old' member nations to decide whether to offer working rights straight away to the new EU citizens of Poland, Hungary, Estonia, Latvia, Lithuania, the Czech Republic, Slovakia and Slovenia – or to restrict entry for up to seven years. Britain was the largest country to open up straight away and was joined only by Ireland and Sweden, with most nations deferring free movement for two years. Germany and Austria opted for the full seven-year block and France for five years. 'The decision has been taken after careful analysis of successive independent studies which show that there is unlikely to be a large influx of workers to the

UK after accession,' Straw, then Foreign Secretary, said in his written statement to the House of Commons. 'Forthcoming research commissioned by the Home Office also suggests that the numbers that will migrate to the UK after accession will not be significant.'

MPs and the media had to wait until the following June to see the Home Office commissioned research, much to the annoyance of the opposition as it was published on the very last day of scrutiny of the EU Accession Bill, giving little time for it to be analysed. The researchers from University College London concluded that between 5,000 and 13,000 people from the new member nations would come to Britain each year. One of the key factors leading to the figures was the low number of people who came to live in Britain following the previous expansions of the EU to include Greece in 1981, and Spain and Portugal in 1986, although there had been restrictions on nationals coming to work from all three countries for six years. 'It is predicted ... that there will be only a small increase in the total number of those migrating from eastern to western Europe – whether to visit, to study or to reside – and that the number coming here to seek employment will be minimal,' Beverley Hughes, the Immigration Minister, told MPs.[126] Richard Spring, for the opposition, argued that it would be far more prudent to put restrictions on the new workers for at least two years, just to see how things played out after the historic enlargement of the EU to include the former Communist countries. 'I believe that the government's policy announcement was well meaning but premature – it would be wise of them to reconsider and wait a bit, as many of our European partners have done,' Spring said. Hughes replied that it was 'important that we send as positive a signal as possible – not just as a government, but as a whole Parliament – to all the acceding countries' and avoid treating their nationals as 'second-class citizens'.[127] In the end, Spring did not force a vote on restrictions. 'The Minister has said that safeguards are in place … I accept them and I am grateful to her for that. However, we will want to monitor them carefully. Having said that, I endorse entirely her point that we want to send out a positive message to the accession countries,' he said.

The forecasts of new arrivals from the former Eastern bloc proved hopelessly wrong. An average of 170,000 long-term migrants – those staying more than twelve months – came to Britain every year from 2004 to 2011. Polish communities sprung up around the country, the UK Independence Party made reinstating border controls one of its main rallying cries and by 2015 there were 3.3 million EU citizens living in the UK, a rise of about 2 million on 2003.[128] Failing to apply temporary restrictions on the new EU citizens had been a 'spectacular mistake', Jack Straw admitted in November 2013. 'Net migration reached close to a quarter of a million at its peak in 2010. Lots of red faces, mine included,' he wrote. In fact, it was not yet the peak. Britain imposed the full seven years of restrictions on workers from Bulgaria and Romania, which joined the EU in 2007, and there was another surge in arrivals after they became eligible for full free movement in 2014. There were 828,000 registrations of foreign citizens for national insurance numbers in 2015, of which 630,000 were for EU nationals, up 40,000 or 7 per cent on 2014.[129] The highest number of EU registrations was from Romania (170,000) followed by Poland (111,000). The second-highest annual level ever of net immigration of 333,000 people was announced just four weeks before the EU referendum vote. Of these, 184,000 net arrivals came from EU countries. A vote to stay in the EU would mean 'kissing goodbye permanently to control of immigration', said Boris Johnson, the leading voice of the Leave campaign. While he said he was pro-immigration, there was 'no public consent for the scale of immigration we are seeing' and the situation was 'completely out of control'. Downing Street's response was to say that 'of course people rightly have concerns on immigration but the PM's view is very clearly that wrecking the economy and destroying jobs by getting rid of our privileged access to the world's biggest market is not the answer'. Philip Collins, the former Labour speech writer, wrote in February 2016 that:

> a report by Mercer, a human resources consultancy, this week showed that the British-born workforce has passed its numerical peak. Britain now has a larger body of retired people than ever before. This is the first time since 1850 that the overall British population is growing faster than the available workforce. Importing labour has not been a

cavalier policy choice foisted on the nation by cosmopoli-
tan liberals hoping for multicultural bliss. It has been a way
of paying the bills.[130]

The free movement of citizens to travel, work and live in another member country is one obvious way that the EU im-
pacted Britain. During the first three decades of the twentieth
century the UK experienced net emigration of around 80,000
a year, according to the House of Commons Library.[131] For the
next three decades, from 1931 to 1961, the flow of migration
turned, with average net immigration of around 19,000 a year.
Net emigration returned between 1961 and 1981 but at lower
levels than earlier in the century, averaging around 20,000
a year. After 1991, annual net migration began to increase,
reaching historically high levels of greater than 100,000 a
year every year since 1998. Although this coincided with the
overthrow of Communism and the opening of borders by the
poorer Eastern European countries, the figures consistently
show that there were more non-EU nationals coming to live
in Britain than EU citizens. In 2015, 13 per cent of people
migrating to the UK were British nationals, 43 per cent
(269,000) were nationals of other EU countries and 44 per
cent (279,000) were nationals of non-EU countries. Between
1993 and 2015, the foreign-born population in the UK more
than doubled from 3.8 million to around 8.7 million.[132] While
more than half were born outside the EU, there were some
quirks in the figures. A study by the Migration Observatory at

Oxford University in 2013 found that 7 per cent of EU citizens who had come to the UK since 2001 – 141,000 people – were born outside the Continent. One of the biggest groups were 20,000 Somalis who became naturalised Dutch citizens, a process which took five years, before settling in Britain.[133]

David Cameron first set a target of reducing net immigration to below 100,000 in 2010. As the numbers rose ever higher under his administrations, partly thanks to EU nationals and partly to non-EU nationals, he refused to be deflected from the target. Despite the obvious failure to get immigration back to the tens of thousands, the target nevertheless had a powerful effect, some argued. 'Few people were anxious about foreign students or high-skilled labour migrants before the target was introduced. Now they are all part of a problem to be reduced,' wrote Christina Boswell, director of research for the School of Social and Political Science at the University of Edinburgh. 'The fact of the matter is, targets work very well as political messages. We may dislike targets. We may find them simplifying, distorting and in many cases unrealistic. But once policies are framed in terms of precise quantitative goals, it is very difficult to undo these effects.' Cameron's target contributed to the Brexit vote by labelling the number of EU migrants – whether students, doctors, fruit-pickers or *Big Issue* sellers – as way too high.[134]

The key factors determining levels of EU immigration into Britain were the free movement policy combined with the strength of the British economy and the expansion of the EU into Eastern Europe. This coincided with periods of economic weakness in other large EU countries, especially during the prolonged euro crisis after 2008. The free movement of workers was established in the EEC's founding Treaty of Rome and accepted by Britain when it joined in 1973. It played no role at all in the 1975 EEC referendum, when Britain was deep in economic crisis and not particularly attractive to foreign workers. During the lean years of the 1970s and early 1980s, when the UK economy was on its knees, Britain experienced net emigration. Arrivals only increased after the Thatcher reforms helped the economy turn around and encouraged employers to look for more workers. Crucially, the Maastricht Treaty created the status of EU citizenship for all nationals of member countries, who received the right to move freely across the union to live, study and work. The higher numbers came with the opening up of free movement to much poorer economies. Britain had an unemployment rate of 5 per cent at the time the former Communist countries joined, while in Poland it was 18.5 per cent. Latvia had a GDP of €7,700 per capita compared to €23,300 in the UK.[135] This eastern expansion was a long-term policy goal of both Labour and the Conservatives for geopolitical reasons and made many senior politicians on both sides feel obliged to open the UK up to their citizens straight away. Beyond the possibility for restrictions for the first seven years of membership, the EU refused to introduce any general 'emergency brake' mechanism on the arrival of workers from other member countries, despite the clear economic disparities between east and west, in line with the four fundamental freedoms of the single market: the free circulation of capital, goods, services and workers. A key EU directive of 2004 on 'the right of citizens of the Union and their family members to move and reside freely within the territory of the Member States' declares that any EU citizen can travel to another member country visa-free for a visit of three months or for six months to look for work – including self-employment – and can stay for an unlimited time if working or studying or if self-sufficient.[136] They can be accompanied by family members including spouse or registered partner, children under twenty-one and the parents of the citizen and their spouse. After living in an EU country for five years, they can apply for permanent residency. EU migrants become eligible for welfare and in-work benefits only after passing tests on 'habitual residence' and 'right to reside'. Britain's borders have never been completely open to visitors from the EU. The UK kept out of the Schengen Agreement which abolished passport checks on 'internal' borders between twenty-six European countries.

The historically high levels of immigration seen since 1994 led to growing fears that the benefits system was being exploited by new arrivals and public services were being squeezed. The Home Office failed to produce evidence, however, when asked by the European Commission, to show that EU citizens were systematically abusing British welfare payments. David

Cameron attempted to reassure voters by securing restrictions on in-work benefits paid to EU workers through his renegotiation with Brussels in the run-up to the referendum. The right to claim in-work support followed on from the EU's philosophy of equal treatment for all EU citizens, so Brits abroad could benefit from welfare protections and public services in EU countries. Based on its own research, *The Guardian* claimed in 2015 that unemployed Britons were drawing 'much more' in benefits and allowances in the wealthier EU countries than their nationals were claiming in the UK.[137] At least 30,000 British nationals were claiming unemployment benefit in EU nations in total compared to 65,000 EU nationals claiming Jobseeker's Allowance (JSA) in the UK. However, the Brits were concentrated in more generous western countries such as France, where the unemployed received more than three times as much as a jobless French person in the UK. Four times as many Britons received unemployment benefits in Germany as Germans in the UK, and five times as many in Ireland. However, whereas nearly 15,000 Polish nationals were claiming JSA, just two Britons were recorded as receiving Polish unemployment benefit.

The academic research consensus on the impact of immigrants on the labour market is that there is 'no significant association between migration flows and changes in employment or unemployment for natives', according to Jonathan Portes, Professor of Politics and Public Policy at King's College London.[138] 'Since 2014, the continued buoyant performance of the UK labour market has further reinforced this consensus,' he wrote in evidence to the Home Affairs Select Committee in February 2017.

> Rapid falls in unemployment, now down to about 5 per cent, have been combined with sustained high levels of immigration. Nor is there any evidence that immigration has impacted the employment prospects of specific groups such as the young or unskilled. Crudely, immigrants are not taking our jobs ... While the evidence on wage impacts is less conclusive, the emerging consensus is that recent migration has had little or no impact overall, but possibly some, small, negative impact on low-skilled workers. Nickell and Salaheen (2015) find that a 10 percentage point (not 10 per cent, as misleadingly claimed by a number of politicians) rise in the immigrant share – that is, larger than that observed over the entirety of the last decade – leads to approximately a 1.5 per cent reduction in wages for native workers in the semi/unskilled service sector.

Portes added that it was 'hardly surprising' that young migrants in employment made a positive fiscal contribution, especially as they tended to arrive after completing education.

> Broader concerns about the potential negative impacts on public services appear to be largely unsubstantiated: higher immigration is not associated, at a local level, with longer

NHS waiting times (Giuntella et al, 2015), and in schools, increased numbers of pupils with English as a second language doesn't have any negative impact on levels of achievement for native English speaking students (Geay, Macnally and Telhaj, 2013) … This does not mean, of course, that citizens do not associate their experience of deterioration in public service quality and availability resulting from other factors (in particular, cuts in funding during the UK's ongoing fiscal consolidation) with the increased demand resulting from higher levels of immigration. The fact that migrants' fiscal contribution could, in principle, at least provide enough funding to cover their marginal impact on demand is not much comfort in practice if those revenues are in fact being allocated elsewhere, for tax cuts or deficit reduction, as in fact has been the case.

Portes concluded through economic modelling that cutting immigration after Brexit was 'likely to have a significant adverse impact on UK productivity and GDP per capita'. On the question of whether EU migrants 'paid their way' through taxes, two studies of those who arrived after 2000 came up with different results. Academics from University College London's Centre for Research and Analysis of Migration (CReAM) and analysts from Migration Watch, the independent research group which campaigns for lower immigration, agreed that immigrants from the European Economic Area made a more positive fiscal contribution than UK natives and a far more positive contribution than immigrants from outside the EEA. The UK as a whole ran a budget deficit, which meant that the population received more in public spending than it paid in tax. The two organisations disagreed on whether EEA migrants contributed enough to be net contributors overall. UCL said in a 2014 study that migrants who arrived in the UK between 2001 and 2011 from the EEA contributed £20.2 billion more in taxes to the public purse than they received in benefits, while non-EEA immigrants contributed £5.2 billion. During this decade, the UK-born population contributed £616.5 billion less in taxes than they received in benefits. The authors calculated the net fiscal contribution by factoring in how much they cost in terms of government funds such as NHS expenses, schooling and welfare benefits, then deducting that from their overall tax contribution.[139] Extending their study back to 1995 showed that the net total contribution of all EEA migrants was £4.4 billion up to 2011, with a net cost of £118 billion for non-EEA migrants. Migration Watch pointed out that the UCL study also found that the annual fiscal impact of all EEA migrants was negative in the final three years they observed. 'What they did not make very clear was that they had observed a downward trend in fiscal contributions across the time period,' the campaign group said. It said it used the same methodology as UCL to analyse the impact in the year 2014/15 of European migrants who came after 2000.

For those who arrived from Eastern Europe there was a

fiscal cost of £2.8 billion, but this was offset by a fiscal contribution of £2.8 billion made by those who arrived from
elsewhere in the EEA in the same period. This made the
overall effect in 2014/15 of 'recent' EEA migration broadly neutral. Taking only these more recent arrivals gives a
more favourable outcome because, like the UK-born, those
who have been in the UK for some time tend to cost the
Exchequer more as they grow older and start families.[140]

Migration Watch added that 20 per cent of the 2 million EEA
migrants who arrived since 2004 were in higher-skilled work.
Of the 1.3 million migrants working here, just over half a million were in occupations judged as 'skilled' by government
standards, with 800,000 in low-skilled jobs. Migration Watch
argued that if immigration from the EEA were restricted to
higher-skilled workers plus one dependant per migrant, plus
allowing for one in three European students staying in Britain, net EEA migration could be cut to 65,000 a year. It added
that using work permits to do this would cause European
countries to require similar permits for British workers.

In May 2016, HM Revenue & Customs released data showing that recently arrived EEA nationals, which it defined as
those coming to Britain between 2010 and 2014, paid £3.11 billion in tax and national insurance and received £0.56 billion
in tax credits and child benefit during the tax year 2013/14.
This gave a net fiscal contribution of £2.54 billion.[141] Migration Watch said this did not prove claims that EU migrants

'more than pay their way in Britain' because the figures did not show the full picture.[142]

> They only compare receipts of income tax and National In-surance with payments of child benefit and tax credits. The same comparison shows the UK general population paying six times more than they get. While on the one hand the comparison does not include taxes like VAT and excise duties, on the other hand it doesn't include housing benefit or any other DWP payments, and most importantly does not include the cost of any public services whatsoever.[143]

The popular concerns about immigration which made it the number one political topic in opinion polls in the months before the EU referendum were not fuelled by academic argu-ments over whether migrants made a net fiscal contribution, however, or whether GDP would fall with lower immigration. Nigel Farage, then UKIP leader, harnessed fears about the sheer volume of arrivals when he declared in 2014 that:

> If you said to me, would I like to see over the next ten years a further five million people come in to Britain and if that happened we'd all be slightly richer, I'd say, I'd rather we wer-en't slightly richer, and I'd rather we had communities that were united and where young unemployed British people had a realistic chance of getting a job. I think the social side of this matters more than pure market economics.

Long-standing suspicions that official annual figures on EU migrants living in Britain masked much higher real numbers were addressed in a report from the Office for National Statistics (ONS) in May 2016. It investigated after figures showed there were 2.4 million new national insurance numbers issued to EU citizens in the five years from July 2010 compared to ONS estimates that just over 1 million EU migrants moved to Britain in the same period. The ONS report said that much of the difference could be accounted for by short-term arrivals – those staying for less than a year – who nevertheless did some work and obtained an NI number before leaving. EU migrants who stayed for less than a year were not counted in the official annual figure. Iain Duncan Smith, the former Work and Pensions Secretary, said short-term EU migrants were taking jobs at low rates to undercut British workers.

> They come in, they do hotbedding in bed and breakfasts and things like that, they then take jobs at much lower rates. This has forced the salaries of people in low-skilled and semi-skilled jobs down so they have suffered directly as a result of uncontrolled borders with short-term migration. I am astonished that a government, my government, can sit here and say we had a pledge to bring down migration to tens of thousands but it is all right then because it does not matter how many people come in as long as they do not stay more than fifty-two weeks.

James Brokenshire, the Immigration Minister, told MPs the government remained committed to getting net migration below 100,000 a year:

> National Insurance numbers can be obtained by anyone working in the UK for just a few weeks and the ONS explains clearly why the number of National Insurance registrations should not be compared with migration figures, because they measure entirely different things. Short-term migrants have never been included in the long-term migration statistics, which are governed by UN definitions. We have always had short-term migrants who do not get picked up in the long-term statistics but short-term migration will not have an impact on population growth and population pressures, as they by definition leave the UK within twelve months [of] arriving.[144]

The figure of 1.2 million British 'expats' living in other EU countries was often quoted but the Office for National Statistics said in January 2017 that the true figure for 'sole UK nationals' – who did not have a second passport – living elsewhere in the EU was 890,299.[145] Not having dual citizenship made these people vulnerable to any measures taken by EU countries against British citizens in the light of post-Brexit decisions affecting the rights of the approximately 3.2 million EU migrants in the UK. The ONS said 189,105 of the Brits in EU countries were aged over sixty-five, more than half of them living in Spain. The NHS paid their healthcare bills – which cost less in Spain than in the UK. 'Many moved to Spain in the first place because it was cheaper to live there, because it was cheaper to buy a property,' Sue Wilson, from the campaign group Bremain in Spain, told the House of Commons Brexit Select Committee in February 2017.

> Many of those people, if they were forced to return, not only would they be worse off financially and be a drain on the NHS and perhaps the housing market, they are also going to suffer with their health, so it is not just a financial impact, it's an impact perhaps with their life expectancy.

EU immigration was one factor blamed for the extra pressure on the NHS. Full Fact, the independent fact-checking organisation, estimated that migration from the EU added £160 million in additional costs for the NHS across the UK in 2014, assuming that EU arrivals used health services at the same rate as people of the same age already in Britain. Slightly more costs than this were incurred by non-EU migrants. However, EU nationals made up a disproportionate number of doctors working in the NHS. Figures from September 2015 showed that 55,000 of the 1.2 million staff in the English NHS came from EU countries, with 13,666 from Ireland, the largest EU contingent, followed by 7,171 from Poland, 6,343 from Spain and 5,659 from Portugal.[146] The greatest number of doctors were from Ireland (2,062) followed by Greece (1,612), with EU citizens making up over 10 per cent of doctors and 4 per cent of nurses.[147]

What would have been the levels of immigration in Britain if it had never joined the EU? There is no reliable way of knowing, although the levels of non-EU immigration have consistently been higher than EU citizens despite governments having much more control over them and, since 2010, being determined to cut net annual immigration dramatically. It simply has not been possible because of the demands of the economy and the right of family reunion for those who become established in the UK. The fall of the Iron Curtain in 1989 would still have eventually led to the opening up of Eastern European nations and the ability of their citizens to travel, even without Britain championing their case to join the EU. Britain already had a substantial Polish community dating back to the Polish Resettlement Act of 1947, which offered UK citizenship to around 200,000 displaced Polish troops on British soil who opposed the Soviet takeover of Poland – and also provided a useful source of labour to help rebuild Britain after the war. David Blunkett, the former Home Secretary, argued that 40 per cent of the mainly Polish nationals who registered to work in 2004 were already in the country illegally anyway. 'We didn't just simply say to Poles coming in back in 2004, just come here, we said we'd rather you come here and work than be in the sub-economy,' he said in 2016.[148] By 2015, Poland was the most common origin of the foreign-born UK population, making up 9.5

per cent of those born abroad, followed by India (9 per cent), Pakistan (5.9 per cent), Ireland (4.5 per cent) and Germany (3.3 per cent).[149]

Denis MacShane, who was Europe Minister when the Labour government decided not to restrict workers from the former Communist countries, and was the son of a Polish wartime migrant, has argued that Britain should try to control immigration from the EU with internal measures or face reciprocal action. 'External controls, such as reverting to Cold War-era travel, work and residence permits, are unlikely to work,' he said.

> Far better is to argue for internal controls, by changing how the UK labour market is organised. Under EU rules no state agency is obliged to hire foreign workers. But successive health secretaries, including those under Labour, have failed to train enough British doctors, nurses and health care workers. The same is true for all craft workers, such as electricians, plumbers, painters, carpenters and shop-fitters. Britain could exercise control by making apprenticeships compulsory for UK firms, as they are in Germany, Nordic nations and other countries where local workers do not feel as under threat as British workers do from European colleagues.[150]

Theresa May's decision to opt out of the EU's single market suggested a new regime of external controls including work permits, however. MacShane added that identity cards could be introduced to police access to healthcare and education, although this would be a dramatic step after strong resistance to Labour's Identity Cards Act of 2006 to create a card led to its repeal in 2010. People in Britain do not currently have to carry any form of ID, unlike citizens in other EU countries.

The most widely discussed alternative immigration system for EU nationals during the referendum campaign was a points-based system similar to that in Australia, although critics pointed out the Home Office under the previous Labour government ran a version of a points-based system for non-EU migrants coming to Britain and that had failed to keep numbers down. Theresa May was quick to rule out this approach. The Prime Minister said in September 2016 that a points-based system did not give the government enough of a say over who came to Britain. 'What the British people voted for on 23 June was to bring some control into the movement of people from the European Union to the UK. A points-based system does not give you that control,' she said. 'I want a system where the government is able to decide who comes into the country. I think that's what the British people want. A points-based system means that people just come in automatically if they meet the criteria.' A Downing Street spokeswoman added:

When Labour introduced a points-based immigration system, the numbers went straight up. In Australia, they have a points-based system and they have higher immigration per capita than Britain. A points-based system would give foreign nationals the right to come to Britain if they meet certain criteria. An immigration system that works for Britain would ensure that the right to decide who comes to the country resides with the government.

This statement led to speculation that the government was planning a work permit system that would only let foreign nationals in if they already had a firm job offer, blocking EU nationals from coming to look for work. Nor was the Australian system as open-ended as was implied. It publishes a Skilled Occupation List showing the maximum number of workers who will be accepted each year. For 2016/17, for example, the number of qualified accountants was set at 2,500, chefs at 2,854 and secondary school teachers at 8,032.[151]

Stephen Crabb, the Work and Pensions Secretary under Cameron, warned in early 2017 that people who backed Brexit in the belief that it would lead to a cut in immigration had voted for an impossibility. 'For many, a vote for Brexit was indeed a vote to take back control and return to Westminster the full tools to cut immigration,' Crabb wrote.[152] 'The problem is that, set against the popular expectation that Brexit means cutting immigration, there is nothing on the horizon to suggest that achieving any significant reduction is achievable or even desirable.' No minister had been able to point to any group of foreign workers who should or would not be in the country after Brexit, he said. On top of that, the governments of Australia, New Zealand, Canada and India were looking for easier access for their workers to come to the UK as part of any trade deal.

> There could be another rude awakening for the public when they realise that Brexit will not mean a cut in immigration after all. It would be far better for the government to be upfront with the British public now and begin explaining current labour market and demographic realities. The previous pledge to cut immigration to the tens of thousands is, in truth, increasingly irrelevant.

Less than two months later, David Davis, the Brexit Secretary, admitted that immigration levels would not necessarily reduce after Britain left the EU. Some industries were 'dependent on migrants', which meant the level would rise as well as fall when necessary, he told BBC1's *Question Time*.[153]

> The first issue here is to bring this back under the control of the UK government, the UK Parliament. I don't think most people oppose migration; I think most people are in favour of migration so long as it's managed. The point is, it will need to be managed … I cannot imagine that the policy will be anything other than that which is in the national interest. Which means that from time to time we will need more, from time to time we will need less.

Asked whether the target of reducing net migration to below 100,000 still applied, he said: 'I think we will get there, but the simple truth is that we have to manage this properly. You have got industries dependent on migrants, you have got social welfare, the NHS, you have to make sure they can do the work.'

Fears have been raised about the need to set up a 'hard border' between Northern Ireland and the Republic of Ireland after Brexit to be able to regulate immigration and prevent EU citizens 'sneaking in' across Britain's only land border with Europe. But, as Jonathan Portes has written, EU citizens who want to work illegally could present their passport at the border and say they are coming on holiday, just as a US or Canadian citizen.

> Control over how many and which EEA nationals are allowed to work in the UK will not, in practice, be applied at the border in the vast majority of cases. As with other non-visa nationals, like Americans or Australians, it will be applied in the workplace; employers will have to verify that EEA nationals are entitled to work in the UK, just as they currently do for non-EEA nationals ... Why would someone who plans to work illegally in the UK go via Dublin when she can simply fly to Stansted? There will be issues relating to people coming via Ireland (third country nationals, as now, and security concerns) but we won't be controlling migration on the Irish border. The need for

control on movements of goods (assuming we leave the
Customs Union) is a much more difficult issue.[154]

The future of EU nationals currently in Britain and the
system for dealing with those wanting to come in the future
will be settled in legislation separate from the Great Repeal
Bill, which incorporates EU legal acts into British law, the
Home Secretary said in February 2017. Amber Rudd wrote
to Conservative MPs ahead of voting on the Brexit Bill,
which had faced unsuccessful opposition amendments to
try to force the government to grant British citizenship to
all EU nationals living in the country. 'The Great Repeal
Bill will not change our immigration system,' she wrote. 'This
will be done through a separate Immigration Bill and subsequent secondary legislation so nothing will change for any
EU citizen, whether already resident in the UK or moving
from the EU, without Parliament's approval.' The Immigration Bill with the government's plans for a new immigration
system was set to be published in early 2018 so it could
become law before Britain's exit from the EU. Under one
model being considered, new arrivals from the EU would be
given time-limited working visas for up to five years if they
have a job but banned from claiming in-work benefits for
the duration of their stay in Britain. An independent body,
the migration advisory committee, could be asked to decide
how many visas need to be issued each year for workers in
key industries such as software engineering, health and

social care, farming and hospitality, which are heavily reliant on immigrants.[155]

One group of immigrants which may find it easier to claim a place in Britain post-Brexit are asylum seekers. That is because the UK takes part, selectively, in the Common European Asylum System including the Dublin Regulation, most recently updated in 2013, establishing which country deals with an individual asylum seeker.[156] Britain has been a 'net beneficiary' of the rule that the asylum claim is usually handled in the country where the claimant first entered the EU. In 2014, for example, the UK returned 252 asylum applicants to other EU countries and received sixty-nine people. Refugees tend to enter Europe via its southern border states and have to cross several more before reaching northern and western nations. In 2015, James Brokenshire, Minister of State for Security and Immigration, said that 'the Dublin system … has been of great benefit to the UK, enabling the removal of over 12,000 asylum individuals since 2003 to other participating states'.[157] The European Commission is reviewing the future of the Dublin Regulation given the strains placed on it by the massive migrant influx into continental Europe in 2015. If the general rule that asylum seekers are dealt with in the first country they reach survives, Britain may not be able to continue to use it. This would, at least in theory and all other things being equal, make it harder to eject asylum applicants who crossed the EU to get into the UK. Several directives related to the asylum system and guaranteeing a minimum level playing field could be repealed by the UK in order to deter asylum applications, however. These include the Receptions Conditions Directive of 2003, which sets minimum standards of living, including a right to work after a year if the asylum case is not settled, and the Procedures Directive of 2005, which grants free legal help for those who want to appeal their asylum decision.[158] The Qualification Directive of 2004 extends the grounds for asylum in the Geneva Convention and European Convention on Human Rights to give protection where there is 'a serious and individual threat to life or person by reason of indiscriminate violence' in situations of internal armed conflict. In a commentary on the future of human rights in Britain post-Brexit, Angela Patrick, a human rights barrister, said:

Immigration and asylum specialists are concerned that without the reinforcing floor of minimum shared EU standards, a regressive race to the bottom might begin. The political incentives to be robust will be heightened in light of the increasing numbers of people seeking asylum in Europe, fleeing conflict in Syria and other parts of the world. Specialists are concerned that the standards set by Europe in a post-Brexit era are likely to become a ceiling rather than a floor for those set by the UK authorities.[159]

CHAPTER 9

KILOS

S teve Thoburn became the most famous greengrocer in Britain in 2001 when he was convicted for using a set of scales calibrated only in pounds and ounces to sell bananas. The Sunderland trader was found guilty of breaking the Weights and Measures Act of 1985, as amended by the Units of Measurement Regulations 1995, which stipulated that imperial weighing machines also had to show metric values. The Act was based on a 1980 EEC directive which updated a 1971 directive making the use of metres and kilograms 'binding' to 'eliminate obstacles to trade'.[160] Thoburn's prosecution and sentence of a six-month conditional discharge was followed by similar cases against Colin Hunt from London, who was given a twelve-month conditional discharge in 2001 for selling produce only by the pound; John Dove, from Camelford in Cornwall, who received the same sentence for failing to advertise the price of his fish in kilograms; and Julian Harman, also from Camelford, who broke the law for offering Brussels sprouts for 39p per pound without mentioning the price per kilo. Together, they earned themselves the nickname of the Metric Martyrs. Their heavy-handed treatment fixed in the national psyche the image of ordinary Brits being persecuted for sticking to time-honoured national traditions. Closing her case against Thoburn at Sunderland magistrates' court, Eleanor Sharpston QC for Sunderland City Council said: 'We are not, as has been suggested, living in a UK which is sovereign in the classic British Empire nineteenth-century way. That UK is part of political and legal history.' Sharpston went on to become Britain's Advocate General at the European Court of Justice. Thoburn lost his case at every stage of the British legal system including the House of Lords and was just thirty-nine when he died of a heart attack in 2004 shortly after the European Court of Human Rights – a body separate from the EU system – refused to hear his appeal. His memory lives on in a campaign for a royal pardon for the Metric Martyrs and also in the resistance of others, such as Derek Norman, a retired TV and radio repair man and former agent for a UKIP MEP who made the headlines in 2016 at the age of eighty-two. It was revealed that Norman had removed or altered 2,000 road signs the length and breadth of Britain because they had metric distances on them. He founded the Active Resistance to Metrication movement in 2000, a resistance group armed with step ladders, yellow jackets and helmets while removing signs. 'I was an electrical engineer and I was quite happy to use metric units for physics, chemistry and science but I do not see why they should make our everyday life metric,' Norman said.

The Brexit vote revitalised veteran campaigners who wanted to see a return to pounds, ounces, gallons, quarts, firkins and furlongs. Prominent among them was Sir Bill Cash, a long-standing anti-EU Conservative MP for the appropriately named constituency of Stone in Staffordshire. 'Anyone who sits back for a second to consider the realities of life knows we still talk every day about gallons, pints, pounds, ounces and stone – and we all know what we mean,' he told *The Sun* in August 2016. 'Whatever the EU might have wanted, imperial measurements are still very much part of everyday life and I don't hear anybody talking about the length of a cricket pitch as anything other than twenty-two yards.' It was the intrusion of European standardisation into daily life which angered many British people and made them feel as if cherished traditions were under attack. These everyday changes sapped enthusiasm for the European project and made Brussels seem determined to subject everyone to Continental uniformity. Metrication was indelibly linked with the European Union because the system originated in France and was a condition of membership of the EEC when Britain joined in 1973. Yet metrication had been recommended by a committee of British MPs more than a century before the country signed up to Brussels.

The metre and the kilogram were invented in the aftermath

of the French Revolution. As usage grew, the 1875 Convention of the Metre was signed in Paris by seventeen nations and set up the International Bureau of Weights and Measures (BIPM) to coordinate the development of the metric system. Not for the last time, Britain delayed joining the Continental club. This was despite a parliamentary select committee on weights and measures in 1862 recommending that 'the use of the Metric system be rendered legal', adding that 'no compulsory measures should be resorted to until they are sanctioned by the general conviction of the public'. It also said that 'a decimal system of money' should be considered, sowing the seeds for the switch to currency decimalisation in Britain more than a century later, in 1971. The MPs in 1862 unanimously concluded that 'the best course to adopt is, cautiously but steadily, to introduce the metric system in this country ... Your Committee think that no country, especially no commercial country, should fail to adopt a system which will save time and lessen labour.' The subsequent Weights and Measures Act of 1864 legalised metric units for 'contracts and dealings' and Britain eventually signed the Convention of the Metre and joined the BIPM in 1884. In the same year, the British engineering company Johnson, Matthey & Co. manufactured the benchmark metres and kilograms which were distributed around the member nations. A parliamentary select committee urged the adoption of metrication in 1895, but while the Weights and Measures Act of 1896 legalised metric units for all uses, they were not made compulsory. Britain's voluntary adoption of metrication was glacially slow. In 1948, a committee was set up to review national weights and measures by the Board of Trade under Sir Edward Hodgson comprising 'men with experience of wholesaling, retailing, scale manufacture, local government, central government and metrology together with two housewives'.[161] In 1951, the Hodgson Committee published fifty recommendations, including that 'the imperial system of measurement should be abolished in favour of the complete adoption of the metric system over a period of about twenty years'. The government rejected this recommendation but pledged 'as time permits' to give it 'lengthy and most serious consideration'.[162]

Asked in 1965 about 'the adoption in Great Britain of metric weights and measures', Douglas Jay, the President of the Board of Trade, told Parliament that:

The government are impressed with the case which has been put to them by the representatives of industry for the wider use in British industry of the metric system of weights and measures. Countries using that system now take more than one-half of our exports; and the total proportion of world trade conducted in terms of metric units will no doubt continue to increase. Against that background the government consider it desirable that British industries on a broadening front should adopt metric units, sector by sector, until that system can become in time the primary system of weights and measures for the country as a

whole ... The government have therefore asked the British
Standards Institution – and the Institution have agreed – to
pay special attention to this work and to press on with it as
speedily as possible.[163]

Jay added that the switch to metric should happen 'as and
when this becomes practicable for particular industries ...
Practical difficulties attending the changeover will, of course,
mean that this process must be gradual; but the government
hope that within ten years the greater part of the country's
industry will have effected the change.' A Parliamentary
Standing Joint Committee on Metrication was appointed in
1966 and the government followed its advice to create a Metrication Board in 1969 to 'guide, stimulate and co-ordinate'
industry to switch over by 1975 'with the qualification that
if the date proved unreasonable for any particular sector the
programme might aim at an earlier or later date'. The voluntary approach was accepted by most sectors, especially those
concerned with international trade, and a 1972 White Paper
on Metrication noted that 83 per cent of UK exports went
to markets 'that are or soon will be metric'. Even the United
States appeared to be heading for metrication at the time,
although this never came to pass and it continues to remain
the only major world exporter to keep wholly to the imperial
system today. There was continued resistance to metrication
from a few British industries and the White Paper acknowledged there would be no deadline set for abandoning pints

for selling draught beer or milk. It proposed sticking with voluntary and not compulsory change but added: 'It is hoped that all manufacturers will do this voluntarily but if necessary the Government would use their powers under the Weights and Measures Act to ensure that this is done'.

Joining the EEC, however, meant that compulsion was just around the corner. The EEC's metrication directive of 1971 made the use of metres and kilograms 'binding' in member nations by the end of 1976. Although it did not specifically scrap miles and ounces, the six original members of the EEC had been using the metric system for more than a century so it seemed clear that the directive was really aimed at nations due to join less than two years later. The 1972 UK White Paper said that:

In due course, as a member ... the terms of the directive will come to be applied here as well. But we shall naturally need a longer period in which to complete the changeover. Arrangements negotiated with the Community will ensure that units used in our legislation are retained until 31 December 1979. Where there are special reasons they may be retained for even longer ... the implementation by the United Kingdom of the EEC directive gives legal form to a pattern, already firmly established, which is likely in large measure to be achieved by 1975 ... The Government intend to take action to ensure that the marking of sizes and quantities is absolutely clear and will consider how

best the housewife can be given information to enable her
to continue to judge value for money.

Successive British governments since the time of Palmerston
debated and eventually encouraged metrication but only ever
voluntarily until EEC membership introduced compulsion.
Britain won an extension of the 1979 deadline but the 1980
directive declared that 'Community provisions have not overcome all obstacles in the field'. It was specifically targeted at
Britain's traditional weights and measures and set down in
black and white that by the end of 1994 it would become illegal commercially to use the following measures: inch, foot,
mile, yard, square foot, acre, square yard, fluid ounce, gill,
pint, quart, gallon, ounce, troy ounce, pound and therm. It
was this European directive that led to the phasing out of gallons as a measure for fuel at petrol stations. Member nations
were given until the end of 1999 to continue to use certain
terms for specific purposes, namely the fathom for marine
navigation, the pint and fluid ounce for 'beer, cider, waters,
lemonades and fruit juices in returnable containers', the gill
for spirit drinks, the ounce and pound for 'goods sold loose
in bulk' and the therm for gas supply. Under these provisions,
the sale of loose fruit and vegetables without any reference
to metric measures alongside imperial values was crimi-
nalised in British law and led to Steve Thoburn having his
illegal weighing scales seized in 2000 for selling bananas at
25p per pound. The final deadline for phasing out all imperial

measures as 'supplementary indications' alongside metric values was later extended to 2009 and after nearly 200 years of resistance, this seemed to sound the death knell for the whole system of British weights and measures.

Widespread public sympathy for the Metric Martyrs brought the law into ridicule and Brussels into disrepute for its desire to banish national traditions. The European Commission eventually showed itself to be sensitive to the reputational damage it was suffering and put the 2009 deadline out to consultation. It took the German member of the commission to show some sympathy for British sensibilities. In September 2007, Günther Verheugen announced that Britain and Ireland would be allowed to continue using the pint, mile and troy ounce in certain circumstances indefinitely. The acre was killed off but goods could still be marked up in pounds and ounces, or in inches and feet, provided the metric equivalent was also displayed. 'Things such as pints and miles and feet and inches are what makes us love Britain,' said Verheugen. 'We do not want to get rid of them. The idea that you could not go for a pint in a pub in Britain is not acceptable.' The *Daily Express* celebrated with the headline 'EU surrenders in triumph for Metric Martyrs' and *The Sun* with 'UK beats EU in war over pint'. There was still time, however, for one last prosecution with the conviction of Janet Devers – sister of Colin Hunt, one of the original Metric Martyrs – for selling scotch bonnets, pak choi and okra on her market stall in Dalston in east London using imperial scales in October

2008. The government responded by calling for an end to such prosecutions, pledging new guidelines for trading standards officers to prevent local authorities from taking traders to court. 'While individual enforcement decisions are rightly a matter for Trading Standards, we are keen to encourage action that is proportionate, consistent and in the public and consumer's interest,' said a spokesman for the Department for Innovation, Universities and Skills.

Brexit means that British laws enforcing the European directives on metric measures could be repealed. One beneficiary could be the champagne business, with Winston Churchill's favourite brand Pol Roger considering a return to imperial pint bottles banned by the EU from 1980 under a 'packaging of liquids' directive.[164] In August 2016, *Drinks International* magazine reported that:

An imperial pint of champagne was once Britain's most popular champagne bottle size – and the size favoured in all prominent London establishments. Winston Churchill, an enthusiast for imperial pints of champagne and more specifically for imperial pints of Pol Roger champagne, popularised the bottle size in the UK. He believed pint bottles held just the right amount – 'enough for two at lunch and one at dinner'. He was known to keep an imperial pint of Pol Roger inside his greatcoat pocket during visits to blitz hit London. Current EU regulation prohibits the imperial pint with legislation specifying the format and size of sparkling wine bottles sold in the UK – 37.5cl for half bottles, with full bottles at 75cl the next available size. The imperial pint, with a capacity of 56.8cl, would sit between the half bottle and bottle at a size considered by many as ideal for sharing.

Official advice on weights and measures on the government website at the start of 2017 was that:

> You must use metric measurements (grams, kilograms, millilitres or litres) when selling packaged or loose goods in England, Scotland or Wales. The only products you can sell in imperial measures are: draught beer or cider by pint; milk in returnable containers by pint; precious metals by troy ounce. You can display an imperial measurement alongside the metric measurement but it can't stand out more than the metric measurement.

Even a repeal of EU requirements would not mean a wholesale return of imperial measurements in Britain, however. Industry has largely converted because almost the whole world, with the notable exception of the US, has switched to metric. 'All measuring equipment is designed to record in metric,' said Nick Catt, president of the UK Weighing Federation, which represents companies making, installing and repairing commercial scales. 'If you want to be a manufacturing country and want to have a strong connection with

Europe, then you have to follow the European norms and rules. Otherwise it would be chaos and it would be consumers who lose out.' Theresa May suggested that food labelling practices would be changed after Brexit in her Conservative Party conference speech in 2016 quoted at the start of this book, when she said, 'We are going, once more, to have the freedom to make our own decisions on a whole host of different matters, from how we label our food to the way in which we choose to control immigration.' Not even the British Weights and Measures Association, a pressure group which supported the Metric Martyrs, believes in a mandatory return to imperial. 'This is the chance for people to be free to use whatever measures they please,' said Warwick Cairns, spokesman for the association.

> After Brexit I cannot imagine forcing people either to go back to imperial or use only metric. The referendum was 52 to 48. Forcing people to use imperial or to abandon feet and inches would really upset people. I think we should go back to the way it was before 2000 where traders could use whatever was wanted and it never caused any problems. My ideal is that those who wish to use metric can and those who wish to use imperial can.[165]

CHAPTER 10

PASSPORTS

There was something rather distinguished about the traditional dark blue hard-backed booklet bearing the title BRITISH PASSPORT above the royal crest. It stood out from the crowd at international border crossings and seemed to convey a sense of national self-assurance with its unique appearance. In 1988, it began to disappear. Little wonder that the phasing out of this beloved piece of British heritage and replacement with a smaller burgundy substitute provoked such strong feelings. The flimsier standardised Continental version had the front cover title EUROPEAN COMMUNITY and, after 1997, EUROPEAN UNION, in a tangible reminder carried by millions of British citizens that their national sovereignty was literally being subsumed by a higher authority. And this was the main idea. The move to a uniform passport was initiated before the digital age and the modern requirement for computer-readable documents. The burgundy booklet was originally intended to evoke feelings of fondness towards Europe and encourage a greater sense of belonging to the union of nations. Attitudes in Britain towards the European project changed dramatically in the years since the common passport was first envisaged in 1974, however, and one of the tangible results of Brexit – widely proclaimed by the tabloids – was the chance to return to the distinctive blue British passport. Nowhere was this possibility seized upon more exuberantly than in *The Sun* newspaper, which began its campaign in August 2016 under the headline 'Blueprint for Britain: It's time to bring BACK the famous dark blue UK passport as a "symbol of our independence" after Brexit'.

> The Sun is calling on the Government to bring back our famous dark blue passport – as a symbol of the UK regaining sovereignty from the EU. We want a pledge from No. 10 to reintroduce the true blue, ditched in 1988 for an EU-approved burgundy passport. Patriotic MPs are rallying to our campaign for the rebirth of the dark blue UK passport – to show our pride at being a fully independent nation again. Tory MP Andrew Bridgen said: 'A country's passport is a symbol of its sovereignty. As we get our sovereignty back, I'm looking forward to getting my British passport back too.'

The dark blue British passport was introduced in 1921. Five years later, the League of Nations, forerunner of the United

Nations, described the design as 'perfection itself' in the battle against fraud, while cautioning that at 7s 6d it was 'so expensive that many countries might be unable to adopt' its specifications. *The Sun* said that 'in 1981 – eight years after we joined the EU – Brussels demanded all member states should have a "European" passport within four years'. In fact, the idea for a harmonised document in Europe first came up at a meeting of ambassadors to the then nine-nation EEC in April 1974, less than eighteen months after Britain became a member of the organisation. It was put firmly on the agenda when heads of government, including the Labour Prime Minister Harold Wilson, met for a summit in Paris in December 1974 called by the new French President Valéry Giscard d'Estaing. Giscard, a committed federalist, wanted to give fresh impetus to the western European club at a time of double-digit inflation, soaring unemployment and industrial unrest. As happened regularly in the EU story, its leaders wanted to use a moment of crisis to deepen European integration. The resulting 37-point communiqué, agreed by Wilson along with his fellow leaders, put booster rockets under the process of 'ever closer union'. They agreed that 'with a view to progress towards European unity', one of the nine would speak for the others on international affairs; they began to erode the national veto over EEC decisions, declaring that 'in order to improve the functioning of the Council … it is necessary to renounce the practice which consists of making agreement on all questions conditional on the unanimous consent of the Member States';

and they stated that 'the time has come for the Nine to agree as soon as possible on an overall concept of European Union'. Along with all this, 'a working party will be set up to study the possibility of establishing a Passport Union and, in anticipation of this, the introduction of a uniform passport'.

In July 1975, just a month after the two-to-one British referendum vote to stay in the EEC, the European Commission set out the implications of the Passport Union idea in a letter from Christopher Soames, the British vice-president, to the European Council. 'The introduction of such a [uniform] passport would have a psychological effect, one which would emphasise the feeling of nationals of the nine Member States of belonging to the Community,' he concluded. This feeling would increase if the passport carried extra benefits such as the right to equal treatment abroad for all EEC nationals. Presciently, the commissioner warned of potential trouble ahead, singling out one member state for special mention:

It should however be pointed out that the detailed arrangements for replacing existing national passports by a uniform passport could raise some problems of a political nature. This could for example be the case with the British passport issued by the United Kingdom not only to British citizens with the right of abode but also to other British subjects who are citizens of non-member countries.

Undeterred, the heads of government meeting in Rome in

December 1975 decided: 'The European Council is agreed on the introduction of a uniform passport which may be issued as from 1978.'

The Commission realised that the next step towards a Passport Union, the abolition of internal border controls between member states for all travellers, would be a quantum step towards Europe as an 'entity'. It would entrust the vetting of visitors to the member nation where they first entered the Community and present the border to the world as a new supranational frontier. It also raised numerous potential problems around harmonising national visa regimes and other policies like deportation practices. Over the next few years, British diplomats strongly resisted the idea of the Passport Union and made it clear the UK would not join. Five of the other countries wanted to go ahead, however, so in 1985 they signed a treaty between themselves on a boat on the Moselle River at the Luxembourg village of Schengen to create an open-border regime on the Continent. The Schengen Area later expanded to twenty-six nations and was incorporated into the European Union as part of the Amsterdam Treaty of 1999. For the true federalists, this was still short of the ultimate goal of a single issuing authority for a European passport. But as Christopher Soames pointed out back in 1975: 'It cannot be imagined that the Member States would in the near future grant the Community authority to issue passports.'

The days of the traditional British passport were numbered from 1974 but its eventual demise was not just due to the centralising zeal of Brussels. Parallel to the move towards a uniform European passport, the International Civil Aviation Organization (ICAO), an agency of the United Nations based in Canada, had been pushing for a worldwide standard to make all passports machine-readable in order to speed up checks at border posts. The ICAO published specifications in 1980 endorsed by the International Organization for Standardisation (ISO) based in Switzerland which were swiftly taken up by Australia, Canada and the US, leading the European Community to incorporate them into its uniform passport plans. It was the ICAO which dictated that the size of all passports should be 125×88mm. It meant the end of the larger British format. In a resolution in June 1981, the ambassadors of the European Community stated they were 'anxious to promote any measures which might strengthen the feeling among nationals of the Member States that they belong to the same Community' and 'resolved that the Member States will endeavour to issue the passport by 1 January 1985 at the latest'.[166] This specified that the uniform passport would be 'burgundy red', meaning that Britain would have to drop its dark blue cover while West Germany and Italy had to abandon green. Yet it was highly significant that the decision came in the form of a resolution rather than a legally binding directive. This was because the European Community did not have legal authority under its treaties to change national passport law – they could only make a non-binding agreement. As the European Council website spells out in its explanation of common terms:

If the resolution covers an area that is not entirely an area of EU competency, it takes the form of a 'resolution of the Council and the representatives of the governments of the member states'. Among other things, Council resolutions are used 'to coordinate member states' actions … in cases where the Council is carrying out a policy objective with a soft coordination process. In these instances, the conclusions or resolutions are drafted to set up objectives or to assess progress.

In other words, Britain was never actually forced to give up its blue document – successive governments simply agreed to go along with a non-binding resolution with everyone else. This was in contrast to the series of binding EU measures to standardise driving licences including the 1996 directive which first set down specifications for the plastic photocard driving licence. This stated that 'the distinguishing sign of the Member State issuing the licence' [UK, in Britain's case] should be 'printed in negative in a blue rectangle and encircled by twelve yellow stars' on the front of the card.[167]

While almost all EU nations have gone along with the uniform passport resolution, one nation realised it did not legally have to comply and does not intend to. Croatia, which joined the EU in 2013, is fiercely committed to its blue passport as a symbol of its independence from the former Communist state of Yugoslavia, which had a red passport. 'The EU's position is that there is no obligation,' Ranko Ostojić, the Croatian interior minister, told the *Večernji List* newspaper in August 2015. 'Not all European passports are burgundy red, they range from brown to burgundy to dark red. We are not going to change our colour, just add the European Union title.' The British government clearly felt obliged to maintain the EU-style passport while the country was still a member, having gone along voluntarily with the non-binding decision for uniformity in numerous meetings dating back to 1974. A spokesperson for the European Commission confirmed in November 2016 that resolutions

are legally non-binding and there are still some differences between the various models of the passports issued by the Member States. With Regulation 2252/2004 on standards for security features and biometrics in passports and travel documents issued by Member States as last amended by Regulation 444/2009, harmonisation of minimum security features, including biometrics of the passports has been achieved. However, format and lay-out as well as issuing procedures remain within the competence of Member States.[168]

Britain cannot change back to the traditional larger size of the dark blue passport because of international requirements set by the ICAO. The colour could be changed at any time. There is already a modern 'blueprint'. The Home Office issues a passport-style document called a Conventional Travel Document in certain circumstances to refugees, stateless people and failed asylum seekers granted humanitarian leave to remain who want to 'travel outside the UK if you're not British and can't use or get a passport from your country', according to the Home Office website. It bears the national coat of arms and the title UNITED KINGDOM OF GREAT BRITAIN AND NORTHERN IRELAND and its cover is blue. In September 2016, the Home Office revealed it was considering changing the passport design in response to the question from Julian Knight, the Conservative MP for Solihull. He asked whether the department 'has made an assessment of the potential costs and benefits of changing current UK passport types to the old blue style passport'. Robert Goodwill, the Minister of State for Immigration, replied: 'We are considering potential changes to the UK passport after the UK has left the European Union. At this early stage we have not undertaken a detailed cost benefit analysis or made any decisions about what a future UK passport might look like.'[169]

CHAPTER 11

RIGHTS

Jacques Delors single-handedly brought about a sea change in the perception of the European project in Britain when he addressed the left-wing sceptics of the Trade Union Congress on his plans for the single market. The President of the European Commission, a French Socialist, told the TUC in September 1988 that, to make sure everyone benefited from the free movement of goods, services, capital and labour, it was 'necessary to improve workers' living and working conditions, and to provide better protection for their health and safety at work'. It was impossible to build Europe on de-regulation alone, he said. The European Community would be characterised by cooperation as well as by competition. Measures to complete the market should not diminish social protections. The TUC, which was officially committed to withdrawal from the EEC, gave him a standing ovation. Delors made it clear that new freedoms for employers to trade easily across borders would go hand in hand with a new era of workers' rights guaranteed at a European level, which was music to the ears of British trade unions after almost a decade of being bashed by Margaret Thatcher. The next day the *Financial Times* noted that 'while Mrs Thatcher's name was not mentioned in Mr Delors' address, many of his statements ran counter to the policies pursued by the UK Government'. Thatcher's own response came just twelve days later. She also avoided mentioning her adversary by name when she gave a landmark speech in Bruges and declared:

> It is ironic that just when those countries such as the Soviet Union, which have tried to run everything from the centre, are learning that success depends on dispersing power and decisions away from the centre, some in the Community seem to want to move in the opposite direction. We have not successfully rolled back the frontiers of the state in Britain, only to see them reimposed at a European level, with a European superstate exercising a new dominance from Brussels.

That single fortnight in September 1988 cemented a realignment in British politics which saw Labour swing behind the EU while the Conservatives – the party that took Britain into Europe – headed irreversibly down the path of Euroscepticism towards the 2016 referendum. Thatcher and her successor John Major refused to accept the 'Social Chapter' of the

Maastricht Treaty, which ended the right of national veto over social protection policies. Tony Blair signed the country up as soon as his Labour government took office in 1997. The EU has passed measures securing rights in the workplace and beyond, including far-reaching gender equality measures, some of which were set not by ministers and MEPs but by judges sitting at the Court of Justice of the EU in cases referred by member nations covering issues from insurance to pensions.

Britain joined the EEC having already adopted ground-breaking equality legislation in the 1970 Equal Pay Act pioneered by Labour's Barbara Castle. She was motivated by the fight of female sewing machinists at the Ford plant in Dagenham to earn the same as men doing the same job making car seats but who received 15 per cent more pay than their female counterparts. The Act was widely hailed as symbolic of the progressive Labour government of Harold Wilson, although, in principle at least, the EEC got there first. Its founding Treaty of Rome declared that 'each Member State shall ... subsequently maintain the application of the principle of equal remuneration for equal work as between men and women workers'. Legal enforcement of this principle took a while, however, and the EEC ended up following in Castle's wake with its Equal Pay Directive of 1975.[170] It was the first of a dozen directives that enforced and extended gender equality, many of which changed the law in Britain to deliver more social rights. The Equal Treatment Directive of 1976 stated 'that there should be no sex discrimination, either direct or indirect, nor by reference to marital or family status, in access to employment, training, working conditions, promotion or dismissal'.[171] Again, Britain had got there first with the Sexual Discrimination Act of 1975, but Britain's legislation had exceptions such as childbirth, pensions, social security payments and taxation. Brussels added the Social Security Directive of 1979 to require equal treatment between women and men in state schemes for protection against sickness, invalidity, accidents at work, occupational diseases and unemployment.[172] The Self-Employment Directive of 1986 ensured equal treatment between men and women and provided protection for self-employed women during pregnancy and motherhood.[173] The Pregnant Workers Directive of 1992 required minimum measures to improve conditions at work for pregnant women and those who had recently given birth or were breastfeeding, including a statutory right to maternity leave of at least fourteen weeks.[174] Britain has gone much further in national law, giving women who have had a child the right to fifty-two weeks of statutory maternity leave. Where the directive requires at least basic sick pay for the fourteen weeks, British law guarantees 90 per cent of normal earnings for the first six weeks, followed by up to thirty-three more weeks at statutory sick pay levels. The Parental Leave Directive of 1996 allowed all parents to be given at least three months' parental leave and to be able to take time off when a child was sick.[175] It was repealed in 2010 and replaced with a more far-reaching directive, enacted into British law by Statutory Instrument in 2013, extending unpaid parental leave to eighteen weeks.[176] The Burden of Proof Directive of 1997 brought judicial changes so the burden of proof was shared more fairly in cases of sex discrimination against employers.[177] The Equal Treatment in Employment Directive of 2002 defined indirect discrimination, harassment and sexual harassment and required the establishment of equality bodies to monitor and support equal treatment.[178] The Equal Treatment in Goods and Services Directive of 2004 extended gender equality legislation outside the employment field for the first time.[179]

These measures forced British law to change – and often the CJEU later extended the rights further. Another key European measure – the 1977 Acquired Rights Directive – was implemented under the Thatcher government in 1981 as the Transfer of Undertakings Regulations, or TUPE.[180] This was intended to protect the jobs, pay and conditions of workers if their business transferred from one employer to another. However, all 6 million public servants were excluded by the government. The next ten years saw fierce battles with trade unions as public sector workers' pay was reduced and workforces sometimes halved during privatisations. When the dustmen of Eastbourne were given notice in 1990 that they were to be sacked and replaced with cheaper labour, they took their case to the CJEU. They won and in 1993 the Conservative government was compelled to extend the coverage of TUPE to public servants.

Barbara Castle's Equal Pay Act ended the discrimination of having a 'women's rate' and a 'men's rate'. But it left a loophole around the undervaluation of women's work where jobs mainly done by women were paid less than jobs mainly done by men requiring similar levels of skill and responsibility. The 1975 Equal Pay Directive made clear that employers should give equal pay for work of equal value. However, the Labour government did not amend the Equal Pay Act, so the European Commission took it to the CJEU and, under orders from European judges and the threat of fines, Britain eventually prepared the Equal Pay Amendment Regulations in 1983. They were introduced into Parliament by Alan Clark, then Conservative Employment Minister. Challenged by Labour MP Clare Short on whether he really believed in the improved right to equal pay for women, he replied: 'A certain separation between expressed and implied beliefs is endemic among those who hold office.'[181] Tony Marlow, a Conservative backbencher, further antagonised the opposition when he warned:

> The measure … states that equal pay should be given for work of equal value. Any troublemaker or any potential irritated employee is going to pretend that her work is of equal value. It is an open invitation to any feminist, any harridan or any rattle-headed female with a chip on her bra strap to take action against her employer.[182]

Once again, the CJEU would be called upon to enforce these

new rights. Using the legislation in 1986, 1,500 female NHS speech therapists claimed equal pay with the mainly male professions of clinical psychology and pharmacy, which earned about £7,000 a year more than them. The UK tribunal and appeal courts did not accept that the women had a right to equal pay as they could not show a rule or policy that prevented them from entering the higher-paid, male-dominated jobs.[183] In 1993, the CJEU disagreed and the speech therapists won equal pay, paving the way for thousands more claims of equal pay for work of equal value. The British Equal Pay Act did not cover indirect discrimination, but the CJEU ruled in a 1986 case that paying part-time workers less pro rata than full-time workers was indirect sex discrimination and could only be justified if the employer showed it was necessary to meet a real need of the business.[184]

Pensions were also excluded from the Equal Pay Act and employers often required a certain number of working hours to join a pension scheme. CJEU rulings in 1994 forced the government to change the law to ensure equal access to part-time workers. It took yet another battle at the court in Luxembourg to win backdated pension rights, however. In 1998, the two-year limit in the British Equal Pay Act was ruled to be insufficient so the government had to change it to a new minimum of six years.[185]

Besides maternity leave, EU directives and court rulings have led to other rights for pregnant women and new mothers. The 1992 Pregnant Workers Directive added to British law the right to paid time off to attend antenatal appointments. A British woman who was dismissed in 1987 because she was absent from work while pregnant was told by UK tribunals and courts that she had not suffered discrimination because a man who was going to be absent in similar circumstances would have been dismissed too. The case was referred to the CJEU, which ruled in 1994 that, because pregnancy is a condition particular to women, treating a woman unfavourably because of it was direct sex discrimination and was not permitted by the 1976 Equal Treatment Directive. This and another case led to a definition of pregnancy or maternity discrimination in the UK's Equality Act 2010 which does not require any comparison with an ill man. The Parental Leave Directive gave men the legal right in Britain to take time off work to care for a child for the first time, ushering in two weeks' paternity and adoption leave through a Statutory Instrument in 2002. The directive also included a right to reasonable time off to deal with an emergency like a family member falling sick. This right is used by 5.3 million workers, or one in five employees, every year, according to the TUC.[186]

The CJEU has also been responsible for changing the law with equality rulings that were criticised for being counter-productive, such as a 2011 case brought by the Belgian consumer association on gender discrimination in insurance premiums.[187] The court ruled that an exemption made for insurers in the 2004 Equal Treatment Directive was invalid because of the fundamental right of gender quality. There were fears that women would end up paying a lot more for car insurance because insurers would no longer be able to charge young men higher premiums, even though they were statistically more likely to have accidents. However, surveys several years after the ruling became binding on all member nations in 2012 found that men were still being charged more than women for car insurance. Stephen McDonald, an economist from Newcastle University, claimed in 2015 that insurers were indirectly discriminating against men by basing premiums on occupation. His research found that male-dominated civil engineers paid 13 per cent above average for motor insurance while premiums in the mostly female profession of dental nursing were 10 per cent below average. The insurance industry had found other ways of calibrating their charges to make up for the European ban on assessment by gender.[188]

The best-known case of a social or employment directive passed in Brussels to extend workers' rights against the wishes of the British government was the Working Time Directive of 1993, which restricted the number of hours employees could be required to work.[189] At the time, John Major had refused to sign up to the 'Social Chapter' but Jacques Delors sidestepped it by introducing the directive as a health and safety policy, a field in which Britain accepted EU measures – and which was agreed by qualified majority voting. On the day of the vote, eleven of the then twelve member nations voted in favour and just one – the UK – voted against. 'The UK strongly opposes any attempt to tell people that they can no longer work the hours they want,' said David Hunt, the Employment Secretary. 'This measure is not about health and not about safety, it is a flagrant abuse of Community rules … a ploy to smuggle through part of the Social Chapter by the back door.'[190] The Major government brought a case at the CJEU and lost, and Britain implemented the directive under the Labour government in 1998. The Working Time Directive brought in a right not to work more than forty-eight hours a week, four weeks' paid annual leave from work, rest breaks of eleven hours in every twenty-four and at least one full day off in seven. The British government won the right for individuals to opt out from the 48-hour week, helping to avoid some employer costs, but then found that the CJEU went on to extend rights into further expensive areas in a series of cases. The SiMAP judgment of 2000 added on-call time to working hours, the Jaeger judgment of 2003 ruled that time spent asleep at hospital counted as working time for medical staff, the Stringer judgment of 2009 ensured that paid leave continued to accrue if the worker was off sick, and the Pereda judgment of 2009 said that if an employee fell sick just before taking annual leave, he or she could take the holiday lost to sickness at a later date. The British government lost a CJEU case in 2006 after arguing that employers simply had to 'enable' workers to take their rest breaks – the judges said this was not sufficient and employers must 'guarantee' rest periods.

When the Working Time Directive came into force, 6 million British workers got an additional week of paid holiday and some – mainly women – received paid leave for the first time because of the new legal requirement covering part-time workers. At the time, it was estimated that one third of part-time workers had no right to any paid holiday, compared to 4 per cent of full-timers. 'If that were still the case today that would be 2.3 million part-time workers without any right to paid holiday – 1.7 million of whom would be women,' the TUC said.[191] Initially, Britain included all bank holidays in the mandatory four weeks' leave. Trade union pressure helped persuade the government to count bank holidays as extra, with the result that since 2008, British full-time workers have enjoyed five weeks and three days' mandatory annual leave. Around 4 million Brits regularly worked more than forty-eight hours a week in 1998 and after the directive came into force this had fallen to 3 million by 2011, according to TUC estimates. The Working Time Directive was by far the most expensive to the economy of all the EU's social and employ-ment measures, with the annual cost put at £4.1 billion by the Open Europe think tank. Much of this fell on public bodies, including the bulk of the £1 billion annual bill for the NHS for locum doctors required to fill in shift rotas to give perma-nent staff their legal breaks. The next most expensive workers' rights measure, the Temporary Agency Work Directive of 2008, was said to cost £2 billion a year.[192] It mandated equal terms and conditions for agency workers as those granted to employees recruited directly.

These two big workers' rights directives have long been in

the sights of campaigns to cut 'red tape' from Brussels. In the speech in 2013 when he announced there would be a referendum on EU membership, David Cameron mentioned just one specific directive he wanted Britain to banish. 'It is neither right nor necessary to claim that the integrity of the single market, or full membership of the European Union requires the working hours of British hospital doctors to be set in Brussels irrespective of the views of British parliamentarians and practitioners,' he said. During the referendum campaign, one of the leading female Conservative campaigners for Leave, Priti Patel, then Minister of State for Employment, argued that workers' rights established by EU law were bad for job creation:

> If we could just halve the burdens of the EU social and employment legislation we could deliver a £4.3 billion boost to our economy and 60,000 new jobs. Just think of how much more success our economy could have if we had the power to reduce the burden of red tape and replace pointless EU rules with sensible domestic regulation.

This led the TUC to warn that EU membership guaranteed workers' rights, and leaving would put them at risk. 'But which rights would go – your right to paid holidays, your right to parental leave, maybe protections for pregnant workers?' said Frances O'Grady, the TUC General Secretary. In her first big Brexit speech, to the 2016 Conservative Party conference, Theresa May sought to allay these concerns with a comprehensive assurance on workers' rights.

'As we repeal the European Communities Act, we will convert the "acquis" – that is, the body of existing EU law – into British law,' she said.

> When the Great Repeal Bill is given Royal Assent, Parliament will be free – subject to international agreements and treaties with other countries and the EU on matters such as trade – to amend, repeal and improve any law it chooses. But by converting the acquis into British law, we will give businesses and workers maximum certainty as we leave the European Union. The same rules and laws will apply to them after Brexit as they did before. Any changes in the law will have to be subject to full scrutiny and proper parliamentary debate. And let me be absolutely clear: existing workers' legal rights will continue to be guaranteed in law – and they will be guaranteed as long as I am Prime Minister … Under this government, we're going [to] see workers' rights not eroded, and not just protected, but enhanced under this government. Because the Conservative Party is the true workers' party, the only party dedicated to making Britain a country that works, not just for the privileged few, but for every single one of us.

May defied expectations to make the defence of EU workers' rights a core commitment after Brexit. This fitted into her personal pledge upon becoming Prime Minister in July 2016 to 'make Britain a country that works not for a privileged few but for every one of us'. Critics pointed out that one workers' right – to move freely around the EU to look for work – was to be ended by Brexit. It begged the question as to how widely May's pledge on 'existing workers' legal rights' would be interpreted. What about the Working Time Directive, which was brought in as health and safety legislation and damned as 'a flagrant abuse of Community rules' by an earlier Conservative Cabinet member? New loopholes in worker protection have emerged in the self-employed world of the 'gig' economy – where workers have a series of short-term contacts or freelance jobs, such as a food delivery or a car journey, and, instead of a regular wage and employee benefits like paid holidays or redundancy payments, they get paid for the gigs they do. Zero-hours contracts also allow employers to escape some legal obligations towards other types of workers. Yet while her predecessor chose a venture capitalist, Adrian Beecroft, to lead a review of employment law, May appointed the former Labour adviser Matthew Taylor. 'Hardly a day seems to go by without stories of workers being unfairly treated, whether in long-established areas of employment such as retail or care, or through new technology-enabled enterprises,' Mr Taylor wrote in October 2016. 'Protecting our strengths while tackling the weaknesses is the overarching task facing the review of modern employment that the government has asked me to undertake.'

The government's White Paper on the Great Repeal Bill published in March 2017 did make it clear that one safeguard of rights would be jettisoned after Brexit. The EU's Charter of Fundamental Rights, drawn up in 2000 and incorporated into law by the Lisbon Treaty of 2009, pulled together fifty human rights linked to the implementation of EU legislation. Britain did not want to extend its own legislation, the Human Rights Act 1998, and the Labour government insisted on a protocol stating that the Charter created no new rights justiciable in the UK. However the Charter began to be used in some cases referred to the CJEU, notably that of 'NS', an Afghan asylum-seeker, whom the British authorities wished to deport to Greece under the EU's Dublin Regulation but who claimed under the Charter this amounted to degrading treatment. Marina Wheeler, a human rights QC who happens to be married to Boris Johnson, wrote:

This was referred to the Court of Justice [CJEU] in Luxembourg which ruled (in effect, and after some domestic backsliding) that the British opt-out had no legal force and the Charter of Fundamental Rights applied in the UK in precisely the same way as in any other member state. Since then, the English courts have increasingly been urged to recognise and give effect to new Charter-based rights in areas of law as diverse as employment disputes, immigration and asylum claims. So where are we now? Mr Justice Mostyn has put it well. In 1998, the Human Rights Act incorporated large parts of the European Convention on Human Rights – but not all of it. Some parts were deliberately missed out by Parliament. Yet the Charter, he said, 'contains all of those missing parts – and a great deal more'. In spite of Blair's endeavours, he said, 'it would seem that the much wider Charter of Rights is now part of our domestic law'.[193]

The White Paper made clear that the Charter would not be converted into UK law because it 'only applies to member states when acting within the scope of EU law, so its relevance is removed by our withdrawal from the EU'.[194] It added:

Some rights will naturally fall away as we leave the EU, such as the right to vote or stand as a candidate in European Parliament elections. It cannot be right that the Charter could be used to bring challenges against the government, or for UK legislation after our withdrawal to be struck down on the basis of the Charter … The government's intention is that the removal of the Charter from UK law will not affect the substantive rights that individuals already benefit from in the UK. Many of these underlying rights exist elsewhere in the body of EU law which we will be converting into UK law. Others already exist in UK law, or in international agreements to which the UK is a party. As EU law is converted into UK law by the Great Repeal Bill, it will continue to be interpreted by UK courts in a way that is consistent with those underlying rights.

Liberty, the human rights campaign group, called for the government to reverse its pledge to scrap the Charter of Fundamental Rights. It called for an independent audit of 'the human rights protections the public stand to lose' and then a formal commitment that every one of them will be safeguarded. 'How can the government trumpet a "stronger, fairer Britain" if its approach means we'll end up with fewer rights than we have now?' said Martha Spurrier, director of Liberty.[195]

One backdoor method of phasing out EU rights and protections has been ruled out by the government. In October 2016, Grant Shapps, the former Conservative Party chairman, proposed a sunset clause for all EU laws in the Great Repeal Bill to give ministers five years to decide which they wanted to keep before they ceased to apply. However, in a Commons debate on workers' rights in November 2016, the first in a series of key Brexit issues discussed by MPs in Parliament, Greg Clark, the Secretary of State for Business, Energy and Industrial Strategy, pledged: 'All of the workers' rights that are enjoyed under the EU will be part of that Bill and will be brought across into UK law. That is very clear. There is no intention of having a sunset clause.'[196] Nevertheless, Labour remained suspicious. Clive Lewis, the shadow Secretary for Business, Energy and Industrial Strategy, argued:

What we did not hear from the Secretary of State was any promise or guarantee that employment legislation will not, once it comes out of international law, simply go into secondary law. We want to see it in primary law and our concern is that once it goes into secondary law, the government will use statutory instruments to undermine employment law and workers' rights, and that is not what we want to see … Why should we believe that the party that has fought tooth and nail against EU protections for workers and that has dismissed as 'unnecessary red tape' laws that have made UK workplaces more fair and more humane will now be the defender of those rights?[197]

David Jones, the Minister for Exiting the EU, responded for the government by repeating the Prime Minister's reassurances on workers' rights.

We are legislating to ban exclusivity clauses in zero-hours contracts to stop the abuse of such contracts. We introduced shared parental leave in 2015 and extended the right to request flexible working to all employees from June 2014. Those are measures pursued by a Conservative government committed to providing strong protections for workers. We are determined to maintain those protections beyond withdrawal from the EU by enshrining them in our law under the Great Repeal Bill.[198]

CHAPTER 12

TRADE

President Georges Pompidou reversed a decade of French opposition to Britain joining the European club when he gave his approval to the UK's third request to join the EEC. Unlike his stubborn predecessor Charles De Gaulle, who twice rejected British applications, Pompidou accepted the assurances of Prime Minister Edward Heath that Britain was truly ready to turn away from its former global trading partners and focus on Europe. Speaking after meeting Heath in June 1971, the French President said:

I asked the British Prime Minister what he thought of Europe, that is, whether Britain had truly decided to become European, whether this Britain which is an island had decided to come to anchor with the Continent, whether it was prepared, consequently, to break away from the open sea toward which it has always turned, and I can say that the explanations and views Mr Heath expressed to me are in accordance with France's concept of the future of Europe.[199]

The reference to the open sea recalled Winston Churchill's famous angry rant at De Gaulle on the eve of the D-Day landings in 1944 that 'every time we have to decide between Europe and the open sea, it is always the open sea that we shall choose. Every time I have to decide between you and Roosevelt, I shall always choose Roosevelt.' On one level, De Gaulle had to accept that without the Americans, the assault against the Nazis would have been impossible. On another level, he never forgot that Britain looked to the US over France and he blocked EEC entry for Britain in 1963 and 1967. Heath was unusual for a British Prime Minister in the fervour of his Europeanness. He knew that joining the European club would divert trade away from partners across the Atlantic and in the former Empire but his government fought for special deals for Britain's historic Caribbean and Pacific allies in the accession treaty to ensure they had privileged trading access to the EEC's Common Market. A month after Pompidou's remarks, Harold Wilson, then leader of the Labour opposition (who had submitted the entry application in 1969 while Prime Minister before Heath), warned that Commonwealth friends should not be cast aside:

During the previous EEC debates … I told the House of the

Labour Government's dealings with New Zealand after the war, of their spirit of sacrifice in Britain's interest to keep us fed, though it meant rationing themselves, their refusal to exploit the famine by charging higher prices. I said … 'I submit to the House we cannot consistently with the honour of this country take any action now that will betray friends such as those' – that is New Zealand … 'if there has to be a choice, we are not entitled to sell our friends and kinsmen down the river for a problematical and marginal advantage in selling washing machines in Düsseldorf.'[200]

The 'New Zealand issue' became one of the toughest issues of Britain's accession talks as negotiators sought to preserve some of the preferential trading arrangements which had made the distant islands a prolific supplier of key agricultural goods to the UK. New Zealand provided 56 per cent of Britain's cheddar cheese imports and 40 per cent of its butter imports under tariff-free quota systems which protected the Pacific trade route. The EEC, on the other hand, had a butter mountain thanks to the Common Agricultural Policy and was dumping (selling at a grossly cheap rate) subsidised butter in markets which would otherwise have been alternative outlets for New Zealand. There was huge political and popular support for the plight of New Zealand during the accession talks, which made getting a good deal crucial to the parliamentary vote on accepting EEC terms and conditions. Britain's lead negotiator, Sir Con O'Neill, wrote: 'Because New Zealand was small, because

she was far away, because of her support for the war – for
these and many other reasons the way the Community would
treat her had become a touchstone, for millions of ordinary
people, of their attitude towards our entry.[201] In the end, the
EEC agreed to guarantee market entry to a declining duty-free
quota starting at nearly three-quarters of the historic trade of
New Zealand butter and cheese for five years after accession,
with reviews afterwards which extended quotas for butter but
eventually phased out preferential access. Inevitably, given the
focus of efforts on ending tariffs and other barriers to trade
within the Common Market and later the single market, as
well as the generous assistance from the CAP for European
farmers, New Zealand fell off the map as far as trade with the
UK was concerned. In 1960, 43 per cent of New Zealand's imports came from the UK but this fell steadily to 30 per cent in
1970, 14.5 per cent in 1980, and 3.3 per cent by 2016. Britain
received 66.2 per cent of New Zealand's exports in 1950, 34.4
per cent in 1970 but just 4.4 per cent in 2016.[202] The case with
Australia was similar but not quite as dramatic. Britain took
32.7 per cent of Australian exports in 1950, 11.1 per cent in 1970
and 2.7 per cent in 2016.[203]

British exporters and importers shifted to the closer
markets of Europe, accelerating a pattern that was already
developing with the end of Empire preferences. UK exports
to Empire countries made up 49.9 per cent of foreign trade in
1938. By 2014, exports to the fifty-three Commonwealth members were worth £48 billion, approximately 9 per cent of the

UK's total global exports. Imports from the Commonwealth were £47 billion, also around 9 per cent of the UK total.[204] In the twenty years before Britain joined the EEC, the proportion of UK trade with the original six European member nations rose from 13 to 21 per cent. In the twenty years that followed accession, trade with these six countries more than doubled to 44 per cent.[205] It would be strange if it had not grown, given that Britain had entered a customs union with its European partners to smooth trade between themselves by banishing paperwork and inspections at national borders, as well as adopting the Common External Tariff, which protected European producers by imposing punitive duties on overseas producers. Nevertheless, Britain's much greater level of non-EEC trading activity caused problems from the start. The complex formula for budget contributions to Brussels was partly linked to customs duties collected on imports from the rest of the world, of which the UK had disproportionately more than the other member nations. This led almost immediately to British government attempts to renegotiate its membership fee, culminating in Margaret Thatcher's 'I want my money back' ultimatum and the introduction in 1984 of an annual rebate. It was the first clear sign that Britain was out of step with the other members and proved to be an enduring source of rancour as the European Commission tried again and again to end the cashback deal whenever the budget was up for renegotiation.

Britain's focus on its Continental partners not only changed external trading patterns but also had a big impact on the internal geography of UK trade and manufacturing. Between 1970 and 1992, ports in the south of the country saw their share of manufactured imports increase by 20 percentage points from 42 per cent in 1970 to 62 per cent in 1992. Exports went in a similar direction, with ports in the south seeing their share of manufactured exports rise from 47 per cent to 58 per cent.[206] The main port to benefit from increased trade with the EU was Dover, which went from handling 5.6 per cent of manufactured exports in 1970 to 19.4 per cent in 1992. This threefold increase in activity was matched by a similar order of decline in business for Liverpool as EU membership acted to deepen the north/south divide in economic activity in the UK.

In the years following the financial crisis of 2007–08, as the EU nations using the euro struggled to rebuild their economies, Britain's share of trade with its neighbours began to fall, fuelling arguments that remaining in the EU was like being 'shackled to a corpse'. This phrase, originally coined in the First World War by the Germans to describe their allies the Austro-Hungarian Empire, resonated so widely that David Cameron addressed it (and therefore reminded voters of it) on the last day of campaigning before the vote. 'We are not shackled to a corpse,' the Prime Minister told the BBC. 'You can see the European economy's recovery. It's the largest single market in the world.' The EU was the largest single market by population, but the second biggest by GDP after the US. It was also indelibly associated with chronic high unemployment in Greece and Spain, as well as endless rows about how best to make the euro work. The corpse image was invoked partly because of low growth in the Eurozone and partly because of Britain's declining proportion of trade with the rest of the EU. Was the corpse a fair analogy? As far as growth was concerned, the Eurozone grew by 2 per cent in 2015 but by an average of just 0.8 per cent a year from 2005 to 2015. The EU as a whole grew by 2.2 per cent and an average of 0.9 per cent while the British economy also grew in 2015 by 2.2 per cent and by a ten-year average of 1.2 per cent.[207] Thirteen EU countries had a better long-term average growth record than Britain, including Poland (3.9 per cent), Sweden (1.8 per cent) – both outside the euro – and Germany (1.4 per cent), but fourteen were equal or worse including France (0.9 per cent) and Italy (-0.5 per cent). As for UK–EU trade, in 2015, the last full year before the EU referendum, UK goods and services exports to the other twenty-seven member nations were £222.9 billion, accounting for 43.8 per cent of Britain's worldwide total sales. Imports of goods and services from the EU amounted to £290.9 billion, or 53.1 per cent of the grand total. Trade with the EU as a proportion of total activity was in decline, falling from 55 per cent of UK exports and 58 per cent of imports in 2002.[208] The totals were slightly inflated by the 'Rotterdam effect', the goods counted as trade with the Netherlands when in fact they were in transit through its ports, often to a non-EU country. After discounting half of the Dutch trade value, an exercise described by the Office for National Statistics as 'perhaps towards the top end of the range' in allowing for the Rotterdam effect, 43.6 per cent of British goods were sold in EU member nations compared to 46.6 per cent without the adjustment.[209] The EU as a whole was by far the UK's largest trading partner, although on a country-by-country breakdown, the largest single national trade partner was the US, which took 19.7 per cent of British exports and provided 10.9 per cent of imports. While the share of UK trade with the EU has declined since 2002, this was mainly a reflection of rising trade with the rest of the world. EU exports were worth about 13 per cent of the value of the British economy in 2014, just as they were ten years previously. During the same period, exports to non-EU countries increased from around 12 to 16 per cent.[210]

Britain runs a large trade deficit with the EU, importing £68 billion more than it exported in 2015. This has been widely used as an argument that the EU has more to lose from any failure to secure a free trade deal with post-Brexit Britain. Behind the headline figure, however, the EU had a massive surplus on goods of £89 billion while it was Britain that was running a surplus on services to the tune of £21 billion, showing the crucial importance of securing a comprehensive trade agreement open for services as well as for goods. An analysis in October 2016 by Civitas, the centre-right think tank, showed that the failure to achieve any post-Brexit trade deal with the EU would leave UK exporters facing a potential impact of £5.2 billion in tariffs on their goods sold to the EU, while EU exporters would face £12.9 billion in tariffs on their goods coming to the UK, if Britain retaliated with equal border duties.[211] This would be the scenario if trading took place under the basic terms set by the World Trade Organization (WTO) for countries which have not made any special deal with each other. Civitas said exporters to the UK in twenty-two of the twenty-seven EU member states faced higher tariff costs when selling their goods than UK exporters faced when selling goods to those countries. German exporters would have to deal with £3.4 billion of tariffs on goods they export to the UK while British exporters in return would face £900 million of tariffs on goods going to Germany. However none of the individual EU nations faced as big a bill as the £5.2 billion calculated for UK exporters. The research found that the biggest impact would be on exports of goods relating to vehicles, with tariffs in the region of £1.3 billion being applied to UK car-related exports going to the EU. This compared to £3.9 billion for the EU, including £1.8 billion for German car-related exports. Whichever way the situation is analysed, the logic of striving for a broad free trade deal for both goods and services – replicating the openness of the EU single market as far as possible – would be the most satisfactory outcome.

The car industry has become firmly re-established in Britain under foreign ownership, accounting for 10 per cent of UK exports worth £30 billion, with many of the vehicles destined for Continental buyers. In 2014, 57 per cent of the 500,238 vehicles made by Nissan in the UK headed for Europe. The establishment of several major plants went hand in hand with the launch of the EU's single market. Nissan opened its Sunderland plant, now the most productive in the UK, in 1986, the year the Single European Act was signed. Honda began production at Swindon in 1989 and Toyota at Burnaston in Derbyshire in 1992. A so-called 'hard Brexit' and the imposition of WTO tariffs on completed vehicles would mean border duties of 10 per cent, which could hit sales of British-made vehicles to the EU and vice versa. This would be especially damaging for German manufacturers and an incentive for its government to ensure tariffs are avoided as a result of Brexit negotiations. The UK imported 809,853 vehicles from Germany in 2015, with German cars accounting for 52 per cent of the British market. The UK is also an important production location for German car companies, such as BMW making the Mini at Oxford and Rolls-Royce at Goodwood, and Volkswagen making Bentleys at Crewe. Any introduction of tariffs would also apply to components. The Society of Motor Manufacturers and Traders (SMMT) said that 59 per cent of parts in British-built cars were imported, at a cost of £10.4 billion. Of those, about 80 per cent were imported duty-free from EU member states. Some vehicles were particularly reliant on overseas suppliers, with the Vauxhall Astra, built at Ellesmere Port in Merseyside, 75 per cent produced from parts made outside the UK. For example, all alloy wheels, standard on many cars, had to be imported.[212] 'A single car is made up of around 30,000 parts, which can move across the Channel multiple times before the final vehicle is completed,' said Tamzen Isacsson, director of communications at the SMMT. 'We must at all cost avoid tariffs and other barriers such as customs checks, which would cause delays and jeopardise our competitiveness.'

It was a big moment in the process of Brexit when Theresa May announced in her Lancaster House speech in January 2017 that she would not seek to keep Britain inside the single market. This followed the logic of the Brexit mantra of 'taking back control' by giving British politicians the final say over laws and escaping the jurisdiction of the CJEU. Yet the single market had been a Conservative creation. It was largely driven by a blueprint drawn up in 1985 by the European Commission vice-president for the internal market: Arthur Cockfield, a Conservative peer sent to Brussels by Margaret Thatcher. His plan set a timetable for scrapping 300 non-tariff barriers to trade, from technical standards to health regulations. Thatcher approved but was ambushed at a European Council meeting when the Italian Prime Minister chairing the meeting proposed a new treaty to implement Cockfield's plan, which would include a host of other measures including an extension of majority voting so that one or two recalcitrant nations could no longer block reforms. The treaty, known as the Single European Act, came into force in 1987 and its impact was far-reaching – not only enabling the success of EasyJet but easing trade across Europe. There were 300 major company mergers in the twelve member nations that year, compared to sixty-eight the year before. The impact of the single market on Britain's prosperity is hard to assess and involves many 'heroic assumptions', according to one study by academics from Oxford and Berkeley, California, for the Centre for Economic Policy Research in London. It concluded: 'European incomes would have been roughly 5 per cent lower today in the absence of the EU.'[213] One key reason was that politicians could appeal to the spirit of European integration and solidarity to overcome strong domestic resistance to reforms of the labour market and the liberalisation of protected sectors. The single market achieved fewer gains in Britain than the original Common Market, however, because 'the 1980s was a period that saw a good deal of domestic liberalisation and deregulation in Europe, spurred by the examples of Reagan in the United States and Thatcher in the United Kingdom'. Various studies for the European Commission claimed a permanent GDP boost from the single market – of 1 per cent in a 1996 study, then 1.8 per cent in a 2002 paper – while a 2007 analysis claimed a 2.15 per cent rise, with competition for government procurement bringing savings on public contracts of 10 to 30 per cent. In a parliamentary written answer in 2011, Ed Davey, then a junior minister in the Department of Business, Innovation and Skills, wrote:

Available estimates show that the greater level of trade

liberalisation achieved through the single market leads EU countries to trading currently twice as much with each other as they would do otherwise. As a result, the single market may be responsible for income gains in the UK between 2 per cent and 6 per cent, that is, between £1,100 and £3,300 a year per British household.[214]

Only time will tell the accuracy of Treasury forecasts released during the EU referendum campaign predicting that each household will be worse off by £4,300 by 2030 because leaving the EU will cause the British economy to shrink by 6.2 per cent.[215] As *The Guardian*'s economics editor concluded: 'The short answer is that it is impossible to say.'[216]

Would a Britain that never joined the European club have been tempted to join the North American Free Trade Agreement or made some other kind of deals with the US and Canada that similarly enriched the British economy? Again, it is impossible to say – but in 1998, Newt Gingrich, then Speaker of the US House of Representatives, showed both his lack of understanding of the EU system and the possibility that Britain could have joined a North Atlantic trade pact by writing: 'If, as appears likely, there is a movement in the US Congress, as there had been in the Parliament of Canada, to offer Britain some associate status in the North American Free Trade Agreement, I would support it.'[217] NAFTA has not created its own common body of law and settles disputes through national courts or five-member panels drawn from the two countries involved. As *The Economist* observed at the time:

NAFTA looks like the kind of arrangement that Britain has always wanted the European Union to become ... There is just one snag. On joining the European Union, Britain agreed to conduct all trade negotiation under the aegis of the EU. It would be illegal under European law for the British to make a unilateral decision to join NAFTA.[218]

As international trade is an exclusive power of the EU, Brussels represented Britain at the WTO in Geneva and negotiated free trade deals with other countries on its behalf. The EU has a good record in lowering barriers to trade with neighbouring countries but failed to strike many blockbuster international deals further afield. In early 2017 it was close to completing its first comprehensive trade agreement with a non-EU member of the G8 most advanced economies – Canada – and was hoping to reach general agreement with Japan. The British economy was forecast to benefit from the Canada deal by £1.3 billion a year. From the wider G20, the EU had deals with only South Korea and Turkey. The South Korean deal came into force in 2011 and immediately boosted British trade. UK goods exports grew by 82 per cent in 2012 to £4.9 billion and services by 5 per cent to £1.5 billion. The EU had focused its efforts on the WTO's 'Doha Round' attempt to strike a global deal lowering trade barriers, which began in

2001 but ultimately failed. In the meantime, other advanced countries continued to forge bilateral agreements. The biggest potential prize was a trade deal with the US and the latest attempt, called the Transatlantic Trade and Investment Partnership (TTIP), was launched in 2013 but stumbled, partly amid popular opposition in France and Germany over fears that too much power would be handed to American corporations to override public policy using TTIP's investor dispute settlement measures, and partly amid resistance in the US Congress. TTIP was forecast to boost British exports to the US by between 1.2 and 2.9 per cent and benefit the British economy by £4–10 billion a year.[219] These benefits may yet be realised. While President Trump has shown his disinterest in multilateral trade deals, he was extremely positive about the chances of a bilateral deal with the UK. This directly contradicted President Obama's warning during the referendum campaign that leaving the EU would send Britain to 'the back of the queue' for a deal with the US, a suspiciously British expression which was seen as a scare tactic to encourage voters to reject Brexit. The day before May's Lancaster House speech, Trump was asked in an interview with *The Times* whether he would move quickly to seal a new trade deal with the UK. He replied: 'Absolutely, very quickly. I'm a big fan of the UK, we're gonna work very hard to get it done quickly and done properly. Good for both sides … we're gonna get something done very quickly.'[220]

The next day, May expanded on her vision of Global

Britain, explaining that 'many in Britain have always felt that the United Kingdom's place in the European Union came at the expense of our global ties, and of a bolder embrace of free trade with the wider world'. She added:

Since joining the EU, trade as a percentage of GDP has broadly stagnated in the UK. That is why it is time for Britain to get out into the world and rediscover its role as a great, global, trading nation. This is such a priority for me that when I became Prime Minister I established, for the first time, a Department for International Trade, led by Liam Fox. We want to get out into the wider world, to trade and do business all around the globe. Countries including China, Brazil, and the Gulf States have already expressed their interest in striking trade deals with us. We have started discussions on future trade ties with countries like Australia, New Zealand and India. And President-Elect Trump has said Britain is not 'at the back of the queue' for a trade deal with the United States, the world's biggest economy, but front of the line.

May added that full membership of the EU's Customs Union 'prevents us from negotiating our own comprehensive trade deals' and so Britain would need to leave the Common Commercial Policy and Common External Tariff in order to be able to negotiate trade agreements. She added that she wanted Britain to be 'free to establish our own tariff schedules at the World Trade Organization, meaning we can reach new trade agreements not just with the European Union but with old friends and new allies from outside Europe too'. May's decision to take Brexit Britain out of the single market and Common External Tariff, effectively exiting the EU Customs Union, have raised fears about the impact on relations between Northern Ireland and the Republic of Ireland – the UK's only land border with an EU nation. The latest technology using vehicle number-plate recognition cameras may be able to help monitor goods in transit and avoid the re-imposition of border checkpoints. Any increase in more intrusive security measures could reignite tensions in a region which suffered conflict for three decades from the late 1960s until the Good Friday Agreement of 1998. The disappearance of a 'hard border' together with the improved economic situation since 1998 have contributed to building peace. Edward Heath believed that EEC entry for the UK and Ireland at the first attempt in the early 1960s, opening the border to trade and increasing prosperity, could even have changed the course of history. In 1972, he told the BBC:

> I hoped in 1961 the [EEC] negotiations would be successful and then there would be an improvement in the standard of living in southern Ireland and gradually the differences would disappear between Northern Ireland and southern Ireland, and we would all be members of one community, and things which are important today would become

much less important. The border would become less important because there wouldn't be the differences between the two sides ... but this, alas, didn't happen because of the [French] veto. And now today it is going to be much more difficult.[221]

These words were spoken during a momentous week in British history, just two days after the signing of the EEC accession treaty and six days before fourteen unarmed people were killed by British soldiers during a march against internment in Northern Ireland on what became known as Bloody Sunday.

Another factor holding up the TTIP deal was the difficulty of finding common ground on agriculture. The EU, as this book has shown, has a raft of animal protection measures which could put European farmers at a competitive disadvantage in the face of large-scale US methods. The EU was also generally hostile to genetically modified crops and hormone-enriched beef. As covered in the Farming chapter, the National Farmers' Union appeared open to US production methods. Tom Vilsack, the former US Agriculture Secretary who heads the US Dairy Export Council, said he thought agriculture issues with the UK would be less difficult to resolve than with the EU as a whole.

I think the [Trump] administration might have an easier time with the UK because some of the agricultural issues ... aren't necessarily the gap between the UK and US. On

agriculture issues it's not as deep as it is with some of the
other members of the EU. So it provides them an option
to basically move forward in that part of the world, and
perhaps do that in a way that is a little bit easier than an
overall agreement with twenty-seven [EU member states].
What I experienced as I travelled through the EU and
talked to EU members ... We may find very strong feelings
about ... hormones in beef, or we may find no interest in
hormones in beef but a really strong interest in biotech.
I think in terms of my conversations with the UK, there
was a willingness to sort of work around and work through
those issues.[222]

May also used her Lancaster House speech to name-check the
organisation of Anglophone countries which some believe
could provide an alternative trading bloc for Britain when she
said: 'Even now as we prepare to leave the EU, we are planning
for the next biennial Commonwealth Heads of Government
meeting in 2018 – a reminder of our unique and proud global
relationships.' In February 2017, eighty figures from Britain's
Commonwealth community signed a letter organised by the
Vote Leave campaign urging the UK to quit the EU.[223]

As patriotic Britons of Commonwealth backgrounds, we
saw the EU renegotiation as an opportunity to rediscover
Britain's global vocation. As long as Britain's trade policy
is controlled by the EU, we cannot sign bilateral free trade

agreements with Pakistan, India, Bangladesh, Australia, New Zealand or for that matter any other non-EU state. Vested interests on the Continent sustain a relatively protectionist policy. We have to apply the EU's common external tariff to exports from Commonwealth countries – hurting consumers here as well as producers there. At the same time, our immigration policy forces us, in effect, to turn away qualified workers from the Commonwealth so as to free up unlimited space for migrants from the EU.

Signatories included Pasha Khandaker, president of the Bangladesh Caterers Association UK, and Moni Varma, founder of Veetee Rice, a UK-based food business with a turnover of £80 million a year. Britain Stronger in Europe countered that several Commonwealth figures had urged Britain to remain in the EU. 'Indian Prime Minister Narendra Modi said Britain is the entry point for trade right across Europe, while Australia's former Deputy Prime Minister said the Commonwealth could never replace the trade Britain does with the EU,' they said. Now that Britain has voted for Brexit, could the Commonwealth become an important trading partner?

In 2013, the combined global exports of goods and services from the fifty-three Commonwealth members (including Britain) were valued at $3.4 trillion, or about 15 per cent of the world's total exports in 2013.[224] That compared to total EU exports of around $2.2 trillion. Not only was the total 50 per cent larger, but Commonwealth trade growth was phenomenal. The combined total exports of goods and services of its member countries almost tripled from $1.3 trillion in 2000. Nearly half of the Commonwealth's total exports had come from its developed members (Australia, Canada, Cyprus, Malta, New Zealand and the UK). In relation to the developing countries, the Commonwealth said:

> The share of developing countries in the total trade of Commonwealth members has also increased, from 36 per cent in 2000 to just above 50 per cent in 2013. This has been mainly driven by the Asian members, which account for more than four-fifths of the exports of all Commonwealth developing countries.[225]

For many Commonwealth countries, trading with China had been 'one of the defining features of global trade', the Commonwealth Secretariat said. Between 2000 and 2013, total Commonwealth exports to China increased from $19 billion to $268 billion, and imports from China had risen from $46 billion to $359 billion. Although the Commonwealth was not a formal trading bloc, with no common trade or customs policy, the Secretariat said that 'historical ties' acted to stimulate trade and 'members consider there are significant gains to be made from closer cooperation with and integration into the Commonwealth'. It added:

Intra-Commonwealth trade is estimated at $592 billion (in 2013) and is projected to surpass $1 trillion by 2020. Although it is not a trading bloc, its historical ties, shared values, long-established trading relations, familiar administrative and legal systems, the use of largely one language as the means of communicating with foreign partners and a strong diasporic community all contribute to increased trade flows among members. Econometric results suggest that, when both bilateral partners are Commonwealth members, they tend to trade 20 per cent more, and generate 10 per cent more foreign direct investment inflows than otherwise. This 'Commonwealth effect' implies bilateral trade costs between Commonwealth partners are on average 19 per cent lower compared with those for other country pairs. There exists substantial potential for increasing trade between members, estimated to be $156 billion – that is, about 34 per cent of the current intra-Commonwealth goods trade.[226]

Writing before the EU referendum, the House of Commons Foreign Affairs Committee said some of its evidence 'cast doubt on the suitability of the Commonwealth as a potential framework for new trading relationships' given the political and economic differences between its members.[227] The committee added:

Updating and modernising the Commonwealth framework to engage in a more sustained way with these countries, however – using the full range of foreign policy instruments including diplomacy, trade and development aid – could make the UK more flexible and adaptable in a world where states such as India, South Africa and Nigeria are likely to become ever more important players. However, it is the bilateral relationships with these relatively rising powers, assisted by the historical and cultural links through the Commonwealth as a background, such as Canada, Australia and New Zealand, which should be developed by the UK as it pursues a definitively global role having left the EU.

Baroness Scotland of Asthal, the Secretary-General of the Commonwealth, cautioned in July 2016 that its members would seek tangible benefits from new free trade deals with the UK.

It is a Commonwealth of equals – people are interdependent and, just as people will be looking to get something, they will be looking to give something. One thing that I know a lot of people are looking at is whether the Commonwealth will get back the migration preferences on access to the United Kingdom that they had before, and whether there will be additional benefits in having reignited the Commonwealth family.[228]

Ironically, given the way its trade plummeted with Britain, it is a small country on the other side of the world that has many lessons for the post-Brexit UK. New Zealand managed to strike eight trade deals including with China, Malaysia and Thailand in the time it took for the EU to complete its South Korea agreement. On a visit to Downing Street in January 2017, Bill English, the New Zealand Prime Minister, was happy to let bygones be bygones. He offered to share expertise gained through the decades when New Zealand was forced to wean itself off trade with Britain and forge a new and prosperous future with other partners. 'If the UK wants to show they can negotiate a high-quality trade agreement, then New Zealand is the ideal partner for them,' he said. A couple of days earlier he had been in Brussels, where he agreed to start negotiations on an EU–New Zealand free trade agreement. Standing alongside Jean-Claude Juncker, the European Commission President, English said: 'It is my expectation we should be able to promptly conclude a trading agreement that opens up opportunities for our businesses, small and large, and underscores our shared values.' Once again New Zealand was showing the way – pushing for the best trade deal with old friends in parallel with ambitious talks with new allies.

CHAPTER 13

VACUUM CLEANERS

As one of the country's foremost engineers and most successful entrepreneurs, it was a significant moment when Sir James Dyson called for Britain to leave the European Union.[229] Dyson, billionaire inventor of the bagless vacuum cleaner and a one-time advocate of the euro, said that he regretted the way Britain had cut ties with the Commonwealth, thought a trade war with Brussels was unlikely after Brexit and said the single market was a myth because of numerous remaining language, legal and technical differences. Dyson was also bruised by his own engagements with the EU. His company had battled for years with the authorities in Brussels and the CJEU in Luxembourg over EU product labelling and energy testing rules. Vacuum cleaner efficiency tests did not take account of the very problem that his machines addressed – the loss of suction as the bag filled up with dust. New models were tested while empty, giving cleaners with bags an 'artificially high level of performance' compared with real-life conditions, Dyson claimed. This was the subject of a bitter dispute which saw the CJEU's General Court ruling against Dyson in 2015. It said Dyson had 'failed to demonstrate that there were more reliable, accurate and reproducible tests than the one endorsed by the [European] Commission'. Dyson accused the court of supporting 'unrepresentative tests devised by the [European] Commission with a small group of European manufacturers which in our view disregards the interests of consumers'. A year earlier he had told the BBC exactly who he blamed and why he thought Britain should pull out of the EU:

> I think it is a European Union dominated by Germany, and in our particular field we have these very large German companies who dominate standards setting and energy reduction committees, and so we get the old guard and old technology supported and not new technology. I want to keep EFTA – European free trade – and free movement of peoples, but I don't see that we need to be dominated and bullied by the Germans.

Dyson would later compare the actions of his German rivals Bosch and Siemens to the fraud perpetrated by the German carmaker Volkswagen in cheating diesel car emissions tests. However, the one thing Dyson was not mad with the EU about was the measure seized upon by Brexit supporters and often used during the referendum campaign as an example of micro-management by Brussels and its restriction of consumer choice – the crackdown on vacuum cleaners. This was one of the 'unnecessary' rules allegedly 'costing UK businesses about £600 million a week' that Boris Johnson named at the launch of the Vote Leave battle bus in Cornwall in May 2016. It was 'absolutely crazy that the EU is telling us how powerful our vacuum cleaners have got to be, what shape our bananas have got to be, and all that kind of thing,' Johnson said. EU limits on vacuum cleaner power really struck a chord with the tabloids, making it into the post-Brexit list of 'The EU's top ten pointless decisions the UK can now get rid of' in the *Daily Express* as well as the '10 ways to say Up Yours to EU' in *The Sun*. In 2014, when the restrictions came in, the *Daily Mirror* reported that 'A barmy EU ban on powerful vacuum cleaners could lead to panic buying, watchdogs warned yesterday. Brussels busybodies have pulled the plug on models with motors over 1,600 watts.' The reports focused on the interference of Brussels and possible loss of performance of appliances, rather than potential savings on household electricity bills. 'Britain will be harder hit than most of our European neighbours because hard-to-clean carpets are much more common here,' the *Daily Express* reported in May 2013. The *Daily Telegraph* spoke to Paul Pearce, technical director of the National Carpet Cleaners Association, who said: 'The performance of a vacuum cleaner has more to do with airflow than with the power rating, so it should be possible to reduce the power without affecting the cleaning performance.'

After setting the overall environmental target of a 20 per cent reduction in greenhouse gases and a 20 per cent saving in energy consumption by 2020, Brussels embarked upon an ecodesign crusade. It was aimed at reducing the energy consumption of everyday items in more than forty product groups – including light bulbs as well as TVs and fridges – responsible for around 40 per cent of all EU greenhouse gas emissions. The directive on ecodesign requirements was a classic example of European governance which appeared perfectly logical in Brussels but aggravated British Eurosceptics no end.[230] In Brussels, it was seen as a necessary step towards meeting climate change target goals while to many in the UK it seemed like the type of interfering micro-management which was no business of a supranational body. As Daniel Hannan, the Conservative MEP, wrote: 'It's not that the EU is necessarily wrong about all these things. But how did we reach the stage where such issues are decided by a Continent-wide bureaucracy and then handed down uniformly to 600 million people?'[231] The directive itself claimed market legitimacy in its second clause by saying that 'disparities between the laws or administrative measures adopted by the Member States in relation to the ecodesign of energy-related products can create barriers to trade and distort competition in the Community'. It set no product-specific goals but relied on a series of regulations for various product types drawn up by the European Commission's secretive 'comitology' process, involving committees of bureaucrats meeting in private.

Vacuum cleaners were governed by the ominously numbered EU regulation 666 of 2013, which stated that by September 2014 no new vacuum cleaners should use more than 1,600 watts of electricity and by September 2017 there should be no sales or imports of cleaners using more power than 900 watts. It went further, stipulating that the 2017 models should not make more noise than eighty decibels and the 'operational motor lifetime shall be greater than or equal to 500 hours'. The new rules meant that several bestselling models by German companies Bosch and Miele and US company Hoover would have to be discontinued. But none of the machines made by Dyson were affected. In a position paper on the measures, the company stated:

> Limiting the amount of power that a vacuum cleaner can use will have a positive environmental impact. Dyson broadly agrees with and supports the Commission's recommendations to achieve this. The working documents rightly acknowledge that the implementing measures for vacuum cleaners need to incorporate energy consumption, performance and usability. However, Dyson considers that the Commission could implement more stringent thresholds to achieve greater energy savings.

Dyson's company statement went on to say that old energy efficiency calculations were 'based on the flawed assumption that people vacuum for less time when their vacuum cleaner achieves high dust removal' which falsely protected high watt-age models. But it was the testing regimes the entrepreneur was angry with, not the energy-saving goals. The paradox of a major British company, run by a high-profile Eurosceptic, supporting ecodesign legislation which was lambasted by the country's tabloids drew this response from the European Commission office in the UK: 'Certain UK newspapers like little more than stories which allow them to attack the EU and the "green lobby" while also providing good punning oppor-tunities for headlines.' It added:

> The new rules are based on a tried and tested approach which has already delivered results for all sorts of other ap-pliances and made life easier and cheaper for consumers. A similar labelling system was introduced for fridges and freezers twenty years ago. They now use only one-third of the electricity they did then. Two years after regulations were introduced for television sets, 70 per cent of those on the market were in the top class for energy efficiency. Mar-kets alone won't make improvements in energy efficiency happen, at least not quickly. Innovation often needs to be given a push. Business wants certainty over the rules and to be sure that competitors will not be able to steal a short-term advantage by continuing to produce and market inefficient appliances. The above might be one reason why most vacuum cleaner manufacturers supported the new rules when the industry was (extensively) consulted. The

UK government also supported the rules – Member States could have blocked them had they wished.

The claimed energy-saving gain by the European Commission from the reduction in vacuum cleaner wattage was 19 terawatt hours (TWh) of energy annually in the EU by 2020, equivalent to 5 per cent of the UK's yearly electricity usage. The European Commission insisted that its range of ecodesign measures had cut power usage by the same amount of energy that Italy consumes in a year. But it proved a hard sell to an increasingly Eurosceptic media and public. With regulations in place for twenty-three of the planned forty product groups, including computers, dishwashers and washing machines, the European Commission decided to delay a decision on controversial rules on hairdryers, kettles and toasters during the British referendum campaign. The PR damage was already done, however. 'The British way of life is under fresh threat from the EU as it targets the nation's kettles, toasters and even lawn-mowers,' said the *Daily Express* after the vacuum cleaner rules came out in 2014. 'Another reason for Brexit: Now EU want to BAN kettles & toasters' headlined the Brexit-supporting *Daily Star* in May 2016 while the Remain-backing *Daily Mirror* ran a similar story under the headline 'Why new EU rules could ban your toaster and kettle by autumn'. The popular outcry about EU meddling was not just limited to the UK but included complaints in several member countries and led to a rethink by the European Commission about what was really necessary. Frans Timmermans, the Dutch commissioner put in charge of a better regulation agenda – set up partly in response to David Cameron's repeated calls for less red tape – announced in November 2015 that plans to target toasters and hairdryers were being dropped. Regulations for less powerful kettles would go ahead. An internal EU memo revealed that fears of a hostile press were behind the decision not to regulate for certain products. The EU had been 'regularly accused of regulatory over-reach and intrusiveness in people's daily lives and behavioural choices, when banning products from the market and limiting consumer choice', the internal memo said.[232] 'The strong negative publicity about intrusiveness raises the question whether the estimated but hardly evaluated economic benefits are worth the political costs for the EU and the commission in particular.' The European Commission estimated that 'more efficient appliances are expected to save consumers €100 billion annually – about €465 per household – on their energy bills by 2020'. After Brexit, Britain will be free to scrap the regulations product by product or en masse. Power-saving rules will continue to be extended on the Continent to meet climate change targets but appliance manufacturers could try marketing high-energy items to nostalgic British customers. Despite his support for Brexit, Dyson will not be among them.

CHAPTER 14

VAT

Tampons became the focus of both feminist and Euros-ceptic protest against rigid European Union tax rules in the run-up to the Brexit referendum. Under an EU directive from 1992 to harmonise Value Added Tax (VAT) across the single market, the lowest-permitted reduced rate was set at 5 per cent for all items not already zero-rated.[233] Tampons were moved into the 5 per cent band by Gordon Brown in 2000 from the then standard rate of 17.5 per cent (although this only emerged after his Budget speech because he was too embarrassed to actually say 'tampon' in the House of Commons). The government could not cut VAT entirely without a change to EU law agreed unanimously by all member states. Similarly, it could not impose VAT on areas exempt under EU law such as most financial and insurance services, and certain public services such as education, medical and dental care.

For Paula Sherriff, the Labour MP leading the campaign

for zero-rating, the 5 per cent added to the price of tampons was a 'Vagina Added Tax'. Her amendment to the Finance Bill in October 2015 won the backing of a group of Conservative backbenchers who wanted to highlight the role of the EU in setting VAT rates, leading to the threat of a defeat in the House of Commons given the government's precarious majority of seventeen. Ministers headed off defeat by promising to put pressure on the European Commission to give member states more flexibility, including the possibility to zero-rate tampons. Although this fitted in with Commission plans to review VAT, nothing had been announced by the time of the next Finance Bill in March 2016 so the issue came back with the referendum looming. David Cameron raised it with fellow EU leaders at their quarterly summit and secured agreement that countries would be given the right to cut VAT to zero on women's sanitary products. The wheels of EU bureaucracy turn slowly, however, and nothing actually changed before the referendum although the government was able to claim it had demonstrated its ability to influence decision-making in Brussels.

While VAT on tampons raised £15 million a year, the Treasury received the much higher sum of £2 billion annually from the 5 per cent levied on domestic electricity and gas bills. Domestic fuel VAT was another charge that could not be cut under EU rules. 'In 1993, VAT on household energy bills was imposed,' wrote Boris Johnson, Michael Gove and Gisela Stuart in an article for *The Sun* during the referendum campaign supporting their argument for Brexit. What they neglected to mention was that it was not the European Commission but the Conservative Chancellor Norman Lamont who imposed it. For two decades from 1973, VAT on domestic fuel was zero-rated. Lamont wanted to raise it to the standard level of 17.5 per cent but was forced to settle for the then reduced rate of 8 per cent by a Commons revolt. Under EU rules, if the zero rate is abolished there is no going back. So the 'Three Brexiteers' were able to claim that 'once we vote Leave, we will be able to scrap this unfair and damaging tax'. This was factually correct, but the domestic fuel tax only existed in the first place because it was brought in by the Treasury while it was being run by a prominent Brexit supporter. Johnson, Gove and Stuart promised *Sun* readers that 'fuels bills will be lower for everyone'.

VAT was designed by a Frenchman, Maurice Lauré, and first adopted by France in 1954. Article 99 of the Treaty of Rome in 1957, which founded the original European Economic Community, committed the European Commission to 'consider in what way the law of the various member states concerning turnover taxes, excise duties and other forms of indirect taxation, including compensatory measures applying to exchanges between member states, can be harmonised'. The First VAT Directive of 1967 required the then six member states to replace their systems of indirect taxation with a general consumption tax on goods and services by a deadline of 1970 (extended to 1973 for Italy, the slowest of the original six to adapt to the new system). Britain had a Purchase Tax which was introduced in 1940 on certain products but not services and a Selective Employment Tax (SET) introduced in 1966 which employers had to pay for each employee. The SET was intended to subsidise manufacturers, who received their payments back along with a share of the proceeds from service companies. With his eye on joining the EEC, Edward Heath's Conservative manifesto of 1970 promised to 'abolish the Selective Employment Tax as part of a wider reform of indirect taxation possibly involving the replacement of purchase tax by a value-added tax'. The Labour government had applied to join the EEC but its 1970 manifesto stated:

Unlike the Conservatives, a Labour Government will not be prepared to pay part of the price of entry in advance of entry and irrespective of entry by accepting the policies, on which the Conservative Party are insisting, for levies on food prices, the scrapping of our food subsidies and the introduction of the Value-Added Tax.

The Conservatives won the election and when they brought in VAT with the Finance Act 1972, various items were exempted to make the new tax more acceptable – there would be no charge on most food, drinks (not including alcoholic beverages), fuel, books, gold, construction, bank notes and prescription drugs and appliances. This was where chocolate cakes were made subject to zero VAT but chocolate biscuits were set at the standard rate, leading to the successful legal challenge in 1991 by McVities to the classification of Jaffa Cakes as biscuits. No one in 1972 thought to add women's sanitary products to the untaxed list. The initial VAT rate was 10 per cent and zero-rated items were included in a special section (Schedule 4) while Section 12 on 'reliefs' stipulated that 'the Treasury may by order vary Schedule 4 to this Act by adding or deleting from it any description or by varying any description for the time being specified in it'. Two decades later, the Treasury's discretion would be taken away. Only zero-VAT rates in place on 1 January 1991 were allowed to continue under an EU directive agreed in October 1992 which set the standard rate at a minimum 15 per cent across the member states – although the level in Britain was by then 17.5 per cent and rose again to 20 per cent under George Osborne's first Budget in 2010. It was not the highest in the EU, with 27 per cent charged in Hungary and 25 per cent in Croatia, Denmark and Sweden. Only Luxembourg charged the minimum 15 per cent, although in non-EU Switzerland the standard rate is 8 per cent – a level prohibited as too low in the EU.

There is a strong level of consensus across the political spectrum and among tax experts that the UK should stick with VAT once it leaves the EU. Whether Britain joined the EEC or not, 'We would have ended up with a VAT anyway,' said Professor Richard Murphy, Professor of Practice in International Political Economy at City University. 'VAT was fairly uncommon in the 1970s and now every major economy in the world has got one apart from the US.' American sales taxes, which vary from state to state, were more arbitrary and less efficient, he said.

> There is no comparison between the two taxes. VAT is a technically much more sophisticated tax. It ends up in most cases with the end consumer picking up the charge in the way intended. It is basically an end consumer tax with a quite sophisticated mechanism of guaranteeing pretty much that the interim supply stages do not bear a tax charge so businesses should not bear a significant cost. You cannot argue it is not economically efficient – 150 countries in the world have it.[234]

Successive British governments have used VAT rises to offset cuts in direct taxation through income tax. This has seen the proportion of HMRC tax revenue from VAT rise from 16 per cent in 1980/81 to 22 per cent in 2015/16.[235]

'It has become a much larger proportion [of the tax take] over time, that is clearly ideological and it has been relatively easy to do,' said Professor Murphy.

VAT is here to stay. The areas for debate after Brexit will be the rates, exemptions and scope. Some pointers for future governments were set out in 'Tax by Design', a comprehensive review of UK taxation in 2011 led by Nobel economic sciences laureate Sir James Mirrlees for the Institute for Fiscal Studies. The report said that exempting financial services probably costs the Treasury £10 billion a year and suggested introducing a tax equivalent to VAT which could be based on a finance company's annual cash flow rather than requiring invoices for every transaction. It warned, however, that 'international co-ordination would be desirable to minimise the risk of financial services being actually or notionally relocated in response to the tax'. Mirrlees also recommended removing nearly all zero and reduced rates of VAT combined with redistributive measures to compensate those on lower incomes:

> Our calculations suggest that if almost all zero and reduced rates of VAT in the UK were removed, the government could (in principle) compensate every household to leave them as well off as they were before and still have about £3 billion of revenue left over. Removing zero and reduced rates in isolation would raise considerable revenue and would inflict proportionately larger losses on low-income families than high-income ones. The challenge is to design a reform package that would spend the proceeds on direct tax cuts and benefit increases in a way that is both broadly distributionally neutral and, importantly, would avoid worsening work incentives.

At 2011 prices, Mirrlees suggested a package of compensatory measures for ending all zero and reduced rate VAT, including a cut in income tax of 2p on the basic rate and 1½p on the higher rate; an increase of 3.4 per cent in all tax allowances and thresholds and in rates of all benefits and tax credits, and further increases of 3.4 per cent in the main means-tested benefits (but not tax credits), 2 per cent in the basic state pension, and 10 per cent in child benefit; a £1,000 increase in income tax allowances, which would take 1.5 million people out of income tax; a £4,530 cut in the basic-rate limit for income tax and the upper earnings limit for national insurance contributions. Given the popular furore surrounding VAT on tampons and domestic fuel during the EU referendum campaign, it is hard to see a government rushing into far-reaching sales tax reform. There will be huge political pressure to reduce VAT to zero in these two sensitive areas. After Brexit, VAT will be in the hands of Parliament and, while it will not be the nation's top priority, it will be subject to constant and intense lobbying for specific changes from special interest groups.

Another source of controversy for small businesses were the EU's digital VAT rules, which came into force in 2015. They were designed to stop consumer tax being lost due to multinationals setting up in low-tax countries but have hit small traders such as those selling eBooks, screensavers and website advertising space. Small businesses in Britain previously avoided VAT because of the UK's high registration threshold of £83,000 in taxable turnover. However, the EU rule change means sellers have to charge VAT in any EU buyer's country, at that country's VAT rate, even if the seller is not in the EU. 'Since 1 January 2015, the state that collects VAT is determined by the location of the consumer, rather than the supplier,' said Philippa Charles, head of international arbitration at Stewarts Law LLP.[236]

UK businesses engaged in this type of supply must either register for VAT in each member state where supplies are made, or use the VAT MOSS (modified one-stop shop) to register in an EU-wide scheme. The issue in the UK is that businesses that trade with consumers in the EU, but do not meet the UK turnover threshold ... for VAT registration, cannot use the MOSS scheme, and must individually register in the member states in which they do business – requiring costly advice and assistance in each such state to do so. The alternative is for them to register voluntarily for UK VAT, but this obviously reduces profitability.

After Brexit, 'this scheme may, depending on negotiations, cease to apply for UK businesses engaged in such supply. There is, however, already a non-EU MOSS scheme in place in the EU, and the effect of Brexit may, therefore, simply be to shift UK supplies from one scheme to the other.' Chris Bryce, chief executive of the Association of Independent Professionals and the Self-Employed in the UK, added:

> [The rules] were designed to ensure the right amount of tax is paid to the EU state that products and services are sold in. In practice, these rules are cumbersome and act as a disincentive for some small businesses to trade online. [After Brexit], businesses trading in Europe would still have to apply them, just as they do for the US or Switzerland.

CHAPTER 15

WATER

Caroline Wakefield was six years old when she died from polio caught while swimming in sewage-contaminated sea off Gosport in Hampshire on a family summer holiday in 1957. The tragedy led her parents to start a campaign to clean up Britain's beaches, many of which were notorious for raw effluence piped straight into the water. 'My parents were particularly incensed that there had been so many statements from the authorities saying all was well,' said Chris Wakefield, Caroline's brother, speaking in 2009 about the advice of the day that salt water would kill off sewage bacteria and that the beaches were safe for swimming.[237] Victorian sewer works were designed to pipe raw sewage from holding tanks into the sea, timed with the tides to ensure waste was dispersed. In reality, the tanks regularly overflowed in all tidal conditions, yet politicians were slow to make changes. Parliament refused to allocate national resources to reform the sewage treatment system or even set in place coastal water standards. A BBC *Panorama* programme in 1957 which featured the Wakefields also interviewed a Gosport town councillor who was adamant there was no problem with sewage being pumped into the water just off the coast. 'Everyone knows how cleansing sea water is,' he said. 'As a seaside town I think we would leave ourselves open to great criticism if we spent three quarters of a million pounds of rate-payers' money putting up a sewage farm when we had the sea so handy.' The Wakefields started the Golden List of Beaches, the first guide showing the position of sewage discharge pipes, which later became the Good Beach Guide and was eventually taken on by the Marine Conservation Society. But in the absence of national standards they were unable to bring legal action to stop pollution. The clean-up, when it finally came, was entirely down to European legislation – the Bathing Water Directive of 1976 – which gave countries ten years to designate a list of swimming sites and improve water quality.[238] It set mandatory limits in British law for the first time for a range of microbiological pollutants: total coliforms, faecal coliforms, faecal streptococci, salmonella and enteroviruses. The directive called on governments to list beaches 'where bathing is traditionally practised by a large number of bathers', a loose description which the government sought to exploit to dodge the costs of cleaning up. While France and Italy designated 3,000 beaches, Britain named just twenty-seven at eighteen resorts in England and Wales and none in Northern Ireland or Scotland, 'which was considered to be too cold and so people would not stay in for long enough for any damage to be done'.[239] Popular resorts such as Blackpool – where clean-up costs were estimated at £30 million – and Brighton were not designated as bathing waters and nor was Gosport, where Caroline Wakefield caught polio. No inland bathing areas were named. The European Commission threatened Britain with fines and this moved the government in 1987 to designate another 362 beaches.

Again and again the European Commission resorted to legal action to force Britain to comply with clean bathing water standards. In 1993, the Commission took the government to court when it failed to meet bathing water standards in nine areas around Lancashire's Fylde coast. These improvements were finally implemented by 2001 but only after further threats of fines and court action. By 1995, the UK listed 464 bathing sites for the purposes of the directive and by 2015 there were 633, although there are continual challenges from local councils to remove locations from the list given the clean-up costs this can bring. The government put the price of new sewage plants and work to close or reduce the use of sea outfall pipes and bring beach water up to standard by 1995 at £2 billion. Although Robert Atkins, the then Conservative Environment Minister, stated in a written answer in 1994 that 'current mandatory EC standards give adequate health protection … any additional benefit to be gained by tightening EC standards is likely to be insignificant', Brussels toughened the criteria in 2006 and from 2015 bathing waters were classified as either excellent, good, sufficient or poor with much higher water-quality standards than in the original directive. Beaches labelled 'poor' must either be closed to swimmers or carry information boards highlighting the health risks. With thirty-one sites given this lowest rating in 2015 (4.9 per cent of all swimming areas), Britain had the highest proportion of 'poor' bathing waters in the EU, according to the European Environment Agency's annual report.[240] This also showed that Britain came twenty-sixth out of the twenty-eight member nations for the proportion of 'excellent' rated bathing waters, with 59.6 per cent achieving the highest standard compared to 73.7 per cent in Ireland, 83.2 per cent in Spain and 90.3 per cent in Germany.

The pressure from Brussels to clean up Britain's water was enhanced in 1991 with the Urban Waste Water Directive, which laid down minimum treatment standards at sewage works and controls on discharges in industrial and high population areas.[241] The aim was to prevent the spread of bacteria and viruses and to cut nutrients such as nitrogen and phosphorus, which can damage fresh water and the marine environment by causing excessive algae growth. As recently as March 2015, the European Commission referred the UK to the CJEU over its failure to ensure urban waste water was adequately treated in seventeen areas. In four of the areas – Banchory, Stranraer, Ballycastle and Clacton – treatment was described as inadequate, and in Gibraltar there was 'no treatment plant at all', the Commission said. In ten other areas where waste water discharges into sensitive areas such as freshwaters and estuaries, the existing treatment fails to meet the more stringent standards required for such areas. The areas concerned are Lidsey, Tiverton, Durham (Barkers Haugh), Chester-le-Street, Winchester Central and South (Morestead), Islip, Broughton Astley, Chilton (also known as Windlestone), Witham and Chelmsford.

EU members were given until 1998 to ensure stringent treatment for waste water discharging into 'sensitive areas', until 2000 to ensure appropriate treatment from large urban areas discharging into 'undesignated' waters and until 2005 for discharges from medium-sized areas and discharges to freshwater and estuaries from small areas. The legal case, which was still being considered at the time of writing and could lead to fines, also concerned spills from storm water overflows in Llanelli and Gowerton which were supposed to have been completed by 2000. Considerable investment went into improving the areas mentioned, such as Southern Water's £9 million improvement of Morestead in 2013 and South West Water's £1 million upgrade of the phosphorus removal plant at Tiverton in 2015. A spokesman for DEFRA, which is responsible for enforcing the legislation, said: 'Overall the UK has good compliance with the directive and water companies have committed around £13.5 billion to make the necessary improvements to get all treatment plants up to the EU standards.'[242]

Under the EU's Drinking Water Directives of 1980 and 1998, drinking water is required to have a nitrate concentration of less than 50 mg/l.[243] Another key piece of Brussels legislation designed to reduce water pollution but which brought considerable costs and administrative burdens – especially to farmers – was the Nitrates Directive of 1991.[244] This required member nations to create Nitrate Vulnerable Zones where surface or ground water is at risk of high concentrations of nitrate and control measures are legally enforced. They have to be reviewed every four years. Previously in Britain the control of nitrates had largely been voluntary, based on guidance from the then Ministry of Agriculture, Fisheries and Food, although the Water Act of 1989 enabled the designation of 'nitrate sensitive areas' where farm practice could be legally controlled. The government was reluctant to adopt too much of the Brussels red tape, and took five years instead of the required two before it designated just 8 per cent of England as NVZs. It was taken to the CJEU, which ruled in 2000 that the UK had failed to name enough areas, leading to 55 per cent of England being put under the NVZ system to regulate the use of manure and fertiliser on farms. A review of the directive in 2007 found it had caused 'significant economic costs' for farms in record keeping, building slurry stores, fines for non-compliance and reduced crop yields. A DEFRA impact assessment put the annual compliance costs at £19.3 million, although another DEFRA study suggested reduced costs for artificial fertiliser amounted to between £2.4 million and £10 million a year.[245] DEFRA told MPs on the Environment, Food and Rural Affairs Committee in 2008 that the Nitrates Directive was 'universally unpopular ... because it is trying to impose very prescriptive rules onto something which should really be fairly flexible'. The MPs concluded that:

> There is insufficient evidence to assess how effective the current Action Programme in England has been in reducing nitrate pollution ... The [Nitrates] Directive is flawed. Unlike more recent legislation, such as the Water Framework Directive, it imposes prescriptive rules to achieve its aim. Moreover, the scientific basis for some of the figures mentioned in the Directive is at best unclear. However, despite its shortcomings, it appears to be here to stay.

The overarching EU Water Framework Directive of 2000 required the UK to achieve 'good' status of all water bodies – including rivers, streams, lakes, estuaries, coastal waters up to one mile offshore and groundwater – by 2015.[246] The assessments were based on fifteen 'river basin districts' in the UK and by 2014 in England only 21 per cent of water bodies were classified as 'good' or better against EU standards, rising to 42 per cent in Wales and 52 per cent in Scotland. With the UK at risk of CJEU fines to meet the EU targets, spending to improve water management and quality in the 2015 to 2021 period under this directive was estimated at £3 billion, according to DEFRA.

The Marine Conservation Society believes that European pressure was essential to cleaning up bathing water and improving sewage treatment facilities. 'The fact that the UK only wanted to designate twenty-seven beaches to begin with shows the lack of ambition at the time to protect and improve bathing waters,' said Rachel Wyatt from the society.

When the bathing water directive was revised in 2006 this also led to a renewed effort across the UK to improve bathing waters, with many new partnerships forming to improve beaches which may be 'poor' under the new directive. Advances were also made in the availability of public information. For example, the new directive has led to the Environment Agency providing a wealth of information about the potential sources of pollution and actions to reduce pollution on their 'bathing water explorer'. The revised directive requires that a bathing water profile is provided for each beach. Until this website was made, it was down to organisations like MCS, through our Good Beach Guide, to get this information out to the public. There is also a requirement for information to be displayed on signs at the beach such as the annual classification and information about short-term pollution, something which MCS campaigned for but which has only happened on a consistent basis due to this new requirement. The emphasis on providing the public with up-to-date information has also led to the development of pollution risk forecasting systems which provide daily updates at some beaches – again there is no evidence that this would have happened if it was not for the introduction of the new requirements of the directive.

The UK was also one of the last countries to report the new standards of the bathing water directive, waiting until the last possible year to switch to the new standards, many years later than some other European countries.[247]

The Centre for European Reform (CER) said that successive UK governments sought to use every loophole in the water directives and allowed the discharge of untreated sewage into the sea until 1998, longer than any other European country. The EU directives forced government, water companies and local authorities to spend billions on better water treatment. 'UK politicians could have required such improvements without any pressure from Brussels but the historical evidence does not suggest that they would have done,' the CER said. 'In October 2012, the European Court of Justice [CJEU] upheld a Commission infringement action against the UK for breach of the urban waste water treatment directive, because it continues to allow untreated sewage to "over flow" into rivers during heavy rainstorms, in London and Tyneside.'

The latest EU standards are part of British law through the UK Bathing Water Regulations (2013) and any attempt to amend or repeal would be strongly resisted. Friends of the Earth said it was hard to know for certain what would happen to bathing water standards and enforcement after Brexit given the UK's track record of trying to avoid paying for clean-up measures. 'On beaches that are very popular tourist attractions there are still incentives for local councils to maintain them to a high quality. The issue is more with those beaches that not so many people visit,' said Sam Lowe from the environmental campaign organisation.

> In 2016, the government declassified two beaches as being bathing sites because they were struggling to maintain them. I am not fearing some sort of blanket return to terrible beaches but I do fear that without that accountability mechanism, standards will start to slip because it will not be a priority for local authorities which are strapped for cash.[248]

The delisted bathing beaches in 2016 were Church Cliff in Lyme Regis, Dorset, and Staithes in North Yorkshire. Monitoring for bathing water quality was stopped and the government is no longer obliged to inform the public about the water quality. Both were classified as 'poor' by the EU in 2015 and ministers were being accused of 'washing their hands' of the challenge of cleaning them up by Kerry McCarthy, the shadow Environment Secretary. 'Rather than taking action to clean up the water at these beaches, ministers are leaving visitors unaware of the risks to their health,' she said. Church Cliff beach was taken off the list even though a consultation found seventy-four of the eighty-one people who responded wanted it to remain a designated bathing spot. Steve Crawford, a member of the campaign group Surfers Against Sewage, said that strong regulation was necessary to ensure water companies made clean bathing areas a priority.

'Obviously infrastructure improvements cost a hell of a lot of money… so they need pressure on them to continue to make those improvements,' he said.[249] DEFRA said it was 'committed to creating a cleaner, healthier natural environment for future generations to be proud of – delivering the best possible outcome for the British people. That is why protecting our environment will form an important part of our EU exit negotiations.'

CONCLUSION

The EU changed Britain. It set numerous new standards including many that successive British governments never thought they needed; introduced a host of rights and entitlements; boosted the economy through trade and European worker mobility, which at the same time transformed some communities; put environmental concerns centre stage in sectors as varied as design, energy and transport; and enabled millions to experience Continental breaks through a new era of budget air travel. It ended a range of traditional British practices, although it's fair to say that the acre and gallon will be missed more than leaded patrol, quarantine or raw sewage in the sea near beaches. Millions of tonnes of fish from UK waters were given away while billions of pounds were handed in subsidies to farmers, which helped many to stay in business.

In the British newspaper battle against the EU which began

at roughly the same time that Boris Johnson was a Brussels-bashing correspondent in the Belgian capital, the EU's foibles received pantomime treatment. Outrage was whipped up against measures fully supported by the British government, such as the ban on filament light bulbs, while, contrary to popular belief, the EU did not change the type of fruit on sale one bit through its much-mocked bendy-banana clause. It did overhaul import patterns of the fruit to the detriment of Caribbean producers and, like so many of the changes covered in this book, the driving force was the single market – a key reform driven by the British government. In the case of bananas, the EU's own free trade rules had to be enforced by rulings from the World Trade Organization.

The single market was used as the legal justification for measures as varied as targets to tackle air pollution, improvements to chicken cages and phasing out most of the remaining imperial measurements. Equal treatment for all member nations in the single market was cited as the reason why British animal welfare campaigners could not prevent the export of live sheep, why VAT could not be scrapped on tampons or domestic fuel and why British farmers could not use hormones in meat production. The single market was always a work in progress and the most zealously observed of its four freedoms – the movement of EU citizens – contributed to the loss of faith among British voters in the entire European endeavour. Endless tabloid tales of wasteful spending, vanity projects, superstate plans, the excess of Eurocrats, and voluminous 'red tape' helped destroy the EU's reputation. The EU assisted in this process by consistently failing to find solutions for the flaws in its grandest projects, from the imbalances in the euro to the security risks of open internal borders. Rarely were the technical benefits of EU membership explained in the media, taught in schools or effectively communicated by the EU itself. Above all, it was the narrative of the 'surrender' of British sovereignty, including control over borders, which most powerfully motivated campaigners for Brexit.

The flow of legislation from Brussels was largely consensual – Britain signed the accession treaty, endorsed it in a referendum in 1975 and rarely had significant policy measures forced on it. The death of the traditional blue passport was a classic example of Britain willingly going along with a measure – advanced by the UK's member of the European Commission, who happened to be Sir Winston Churchill's son-in-law – which could have been avoided or reversed by successive governments. Part of the change – the diminution in passport size – was nothing at all to do with the EU but with international bodies on aviation and global standardisation. It would have been a neat PR trick if David Cameron had returned from his renegotiation of Britain's EU deal brandishing a dark blue passport. But he didn't think of it.

Through its regional support programmes, the EU recycled some of Britain's membership fee back to infrastructure and training projects concentrated in poorer areas of the country, with €16.4 billion planned in the seven-year budget period from 2014 to 2020. Occasionally Brussels used a supranational justification to seize control over affairs that the UK wanted to conduct nationally, such as Britain's open skies agreement with the United States and its law on foreign fishing vessel registration. The Court of Justice of the European Union advanced the scope of European law in ways which upset British legislators, from new rights for medical staff for time off asleep while on call at work, to equality rulings on insurance and pension premiums which caused those industries to rethink the way they charged customers. Consumers won important rights, such as compensation for cancelled or delayed flights, while EU-derived food labels gave information on product origins and nutritional values.

The EU introduced a host of workplace rights and equality measures – many of them in the teeth of opposition from the British government – including acquired rights during takeovers, equal pay for work of equal value, paid leave for antenatal appointments and pension and paid holiday rights for part-time workers. The best-known example of a workplace initiative pushed through against the wishes of the UK was the Working Time Directive, which had expensive consequences for employers and benefits for millions of employees who gained extra paid holidays and more time off. This was also among the EU measures which were 'gold-plated' by the British government, with eight days of bank holidays added to the EU minimum of four weeks' annual paid leave. Other domestically enhanced measures include the fifty-two weeks' leave allowance for new mothers, thirty-nine weeks of which is paid – much higher than the EU legal minimum maternity leave of fourteen weeks. The EU even awarded animals the right to be regarded as sentient beings and to move freely around the Continent. Brussels, however, remained in the doghouse.

The EU's reputation was further blighted by the measures it took which sometimes had far-reaching unforeseen consequences, such as the car industry's switch to pumping out harmful nitrogen dioxide in its attempt to meet carbon dioxide reduction targets, or the travesty of a million tonnes of edible fish being thrown back dead every year in the name of conservation. The most relevant miscalculation as regards the Brexit referendum was the UK government's forecast that few citizens of the former Communist countries would come to Britain to live and work, leading to the complete opening up by the Labour government in 2004 while even Poland's neighbour Germany kept temporary restrictions in place. It was a disastrous political judgement in terms of poisoning the well of goodwill in Britain towards its European neighbours and migrants in general, and soured relations with countries which had been firm friends and allies for many years.

Beyond all these legal and political measures, the EU changed Britain's outlook as a nation – its eating and drinking habits, shopping choices and holiday destinations. This was again mainly due to the rules of the single market. Freedom of establishment made it easy for stores such as Zara – most of whose clothes are made in Spain – and Swedish brand H&M to storm the High Street, while freedom of movement made it easier for them to hire design and retail staff from across Europe. Ikea of Sweden set up vast warehouses selling shelves and cupboards for somewhere to put all the stuff bought from these European retailers. Britain remained British in many other ways – three-pin plugs, driving on the left, lack of foreign language skills, the mile, the pint in the pub and the pound were all constant features of life recognisable to any time traveller from 1973.

Brexit will change Britain. The immediate impact of the referendum vote was to send sterling plunging to a three-decade low against the dollar, where it stayed for months afterwards. It also tumbled against the euro. As mentioned in the Flying chapter, this readjustment in exchange rates caused unexpected losses for British companies which had significant costs in other currencies, such as EasyJet. Currency analysts saw the pound as a proxy for market sentiment about the progress of Brexit and forecast that sterling was in for a volatile couple of years during talks on the leaving agreement after the Article 50 process began on 29 March 2017. 'We take the view that sterling is now a barometer between a hard and soft Brexit,' said Kevin Logan, chief US economist at HSBC, in January 2017, when the pound was trading at $1.2442.

We think there will be ultimately a hard Brexit – a hard

break on trade between the UK and Europe and a hard break on immigration. The pound sterling has to adjust to that ... Every time there is new news coming out of Britain we see sterling moving up and down – are we moving faster towards a hard Brexit or are we moving a bit away from it? ... At some point, they really have to make the break. And it may be stretched out a bit but I don't think this trend towards the 1.10 [dollars to the pound] on sterling is going to change.[250]

Another issue that quickly rose to the top of the Brexit agenda was the fate of EU citizens already living in the UK and British citizens based in other member nations. Neither the European Commission nor any individual EU countries would break ranks and agree an immediate deal to guarantee expat rights – May asked Angela Merkel of Germany to do so but the German Chancellor said there could be no pre-talks before Britain formally notified the EU of exit negotiations. May therefore refused to commit the UK to a unilateral declaration of rights for EU nationals. The uncertainty was painful for all those who felt left in limbo – 3 million EU citizens in Britain and a million Brits in other EU nations – and was an early indication of the way certain groups could get caught in the crossfire of the Brexit process. Farmers, fishermen, the nuclear industry, great crested newts, exporters of various goods and services, employers who relied on plentiful EU labour – many endured a nervous wait for the negotiations to unfold. For a range of industries, from fashion to farming and catering to retailing, as well as public and social services like the NHS and care homes, the availability of foreign workers will be key to maintaining production or provision after Brexit. As seen in the Immigration chapter, the demand for migrant workers will not go away easily. Nor did the government really seem to believe that net immigration would fall to anything like its own stated target of less than 100,000 a year, with the Office for Budget Responsibility basing its forecasts for the March 2017 Budget on the assumption that, at most, it would fall to 185,000 by 2021.[251] Britain will have more controls at its disposal to manage its border, but the consistently higher level of non-EU immigration than EU arrivals suggests that reducing overall numbers will always be difficult, especially while the economy is creating more job opportunities than most Continental countries. The possibility of immigration levels remaining high after Brexit was acknowledged by David Davis, the Secretary of State for Exiting the European Union, when he said in March 2017:

> The first issue here is to bring this back under the control of the UK government, the UK Parliament … I think most people are in favour of migration so long as it is managed … I cannot imagine the policy will be anything other than that which is in the national interest, which means that from time to time we will need more, from time to time we

will need less. And that will be in everybody's interests, the migrants and the citizens of the United Kingdom.

May's firm intention to quit the single market and CJEU jurisdiction so Britain could limit migration was a hostage to fortune for some sectors. The nuclear industry was concerned that outside of the Euratom treaty, which requires CJEU oversight, the supply of nuclear materials for energy and medical use could dry up. The aviation industry was worried it would mean leaving the European Single Aviation Market and make British airlines vulnerable to punitive demands, such as giving up routes as a condition of continued access. The financial services industry feared the loss of international companies less able to do business with the rest of the EU from their British base, as well as restrictive terms of continued access for UK finance businesses. Above all, this meant that even a comprehensive free trade agreement could not replicate the ease of transactions enjoyed within the EU, as many prominent European figures made clear. 'The question of whether a country wants to remain a member of the European Union or not has to make a noticeable difference,' warned Angela Merkel, the German Chancellor, in June 2016 after the referendum result. 'Anyone who wants to leave this family can't expect to get rid of all obligations while holding onto privileges. We will make sure the negotiations aren't based on the principle of cherry picking.'[252] Emmanuel Macron, the centre-left contender for the French presidency in 2017, said: 'Brexit cannot lead to a kind of optimisation of Britain's relationship with the rest of Europe. An exit is an exit. I am very determined that there will be no undue advantages.' Professor John Curtice, senior fellow at the UK in a Changing Europe group, said:

In prioritising ending freedom of movement and pulling out of the European Court of Justice, Mrs May is reflecting the two principal concerns of Leave voters in the referendum – immigration and sovereignty. But at the same time she is still trying to deliver what many Leave as well as Remain voters also want, which is continued free trade with the EU. The key challenge facing the government, as the Prime Minister herself seemed to recognise, is whether the EU can be persuaded to strike a deal on free trade on anything like the terms and conditions that she has in mind.

Further afield, the Brexit goal of regaining sovereignty will enable Britain to strike free trade deals with partners of its choice rather than rely on the EU to negotiate on behalf of all the member nations, something it has been slow to do with some of the largest players. But any rush to conclude these agreements brings its own dangers for that prized sovereignty. That is because each trade partner will demand compromises that could impact domestic policy, putting Britain under pressure to scrap long-standing practices or safeguards, for example to accommodate the US view on farm technologies like genetically modified crops or hormone-enhanced meat. Other potential trade partners such as India will seek privileged immigration access in return for lowering tariffs. As Ian Dunt, editor of politics.co.uk, has written: 'With China, the concern will be energy security. Beijing is likely to demand a greater role in the provision of our energy infrastructure … This is the reality of trade talks. Sovereignty will be bartered for commerce.'[253]

As for the impact of Brexit on domestic legal measures, the leading advocates of leaving the EU were mostly vague on the precise rules and regulations they would scrap. One of the clearest views was expressed by Priti Patel, then Employment Minister, who said during the referendum campaign that leaving the EU meant that 'the burdens of EU social and employment legislation' could be halved to save £4.3 billion a year and create 60,000 jobs. She gave one specific example of the EU blocking Britain from exempting self-employed drivers from working-time rules. Although the self-employed are excluded from the 1993 Working Time Directive, a 48-hour week (averaged over four months to allow for up to sixty hours' work in some weeks) and strict break and rest periods for all those who drive for a living, including the self-employed, were brought in by a separate directive on 'the organisation of the working time of persons performing mobile road transport activities'.[254] The EU justified this by the need 'to improve road safety, prevent the distortion of competition and guarantee the safety and health of mobile workers'. Whether this is categorised by the government as a burdensome social

measure or as one of the vital workers' rights which Theresa
May vowed to protect will decide its fate after Brexit.

After the referendum, the Leave Means Leave group, which
campaigned for a swift exit from the EU pointed towards a
list of the 100 most expensive EU-derived laws, drawn up
by the Open Europe think tank, as a place to start looking
for red tape to cut. Using government impact assessments,
the organisation said these 100 measures cost the economy
£33.3 billion a year at 2014 prices with a claimed benefit of
£58.6 billion, which Open Europe called a 'vastly overstated'
figure, especially as the benefits of a yet-to-be realised global
climate change deal were factored in.[255] The most expensive
was the Renewable Energy Strategy, with a recurring annual
cost of £4.7 billion a year, making it a prime target for trim-
ming after Brexit. Ending supplements for renewables like
new wind farms on domestic energy bills might be popular with many voters but would weaken climate protection
efforts. The second most expensive was the Capital Requirements Directive of 2013, at a cost of £4.6 billion a year,
although this transposed into EU law the latest global standards on bank capital adequacy commonly known as Basel
III, overseen by the Basel Committee on Banking Supervi-
sion based in Switzerland (not an EU member state) and
to which the UK belongs separately from the EU. The next
most costly EU directive was the Working Time Directive,
but, as previously mentioned, Theresa May's pledge to maintain workers' rights 'as long as I am Prime Minister' would

seem to prevent it from being repealed, at least for a while. Fourth most expensive, at £3.4 billion a year, was the package of climate change measures including renewable energy targets, which are now voluntary, and emissions trading, which the UK pioneered but which it could drop out of at an EU level after Brexit. Also included in the climate package was a directive on 'the geological storage of carbon dioxide', a new technology placed on the backburner by the government in 2015 when it cancelled a £1 billion trial, suggesting that this EU measure could be scrapped. Fifth, at £2.1 billion, was another workers' rights measure, the Temporary Agency Work Directive, while sixth was the package of building inspection and energy performance rules, costing £1.5 billion a year, which was ripe for pruning. Four further EU measures were calculated to cost more than £1 billion a year. Seventh on the list was the Alternative Investment Fund Managers Directive of 2011, created in response to the 2008 financial crisis, to regulate hedge funds, private equity and other funds.[256] Said to cost £1.5 billion a year, it requires various disclosures, such as leverage levels, as well as rules to combat asset-stripping. Investment companies hate it. The Association of Investment Companies (AIC) argued that 'it is difficult to see that the AIFM Directive provides any material regulatory benefits' and should be scrapped in its entirety, leaving it up to individual companies to decide whether they want to comply in order to continue operating in the EU after Brexit. In a report in November 2016 it said:

The UK would then be free to introduce specific, targeted measures, following consultation, if any were considered necessary. Radically reforming or abolishing the AIFM Directive would reduce unnecessary costs, help deliver keener product pricing for investors and increase the global competitiveness of the UK as a location for funds and asset management.[257]

Next on the top ten costliest EU regulations list were the Motor Vehicle Regulations of 2008, a package of three directives and two regulations said to cost £1.3 billion a year to set standards on noise levels, indicators on vehicles and trailers, and tests on vehicle air conditioning and exhaust gases. This includes the regulation – amended several times – that allowed car manufacturers to pump out higher emissions on the road than in the testing laboratory and is once again under review. Ninth on the list of costliest measures was the Water Framework Directive to bring all inland and coastal waters up to set standards by 2015, with DEFRA estimating the ongoing costs from 2015 to 2021 at £3 billion. Also on the most expensive list, at £1.06 billion a year, was the Data Protection Directive implemented in British law as the Data Protection Act 1998. This gave individuals the right to view the data held by organisations such as credit reference agencies, request corrections and insist that data is not used for direct marketing. The directive will be replaced in May 2018 with sweeping new rights for individuals to safeguard their data following the explosion of social media use, including the 'right to be forgotten' by giving legal backing to requests for online reports to be erased.[258] The new directive will be backed by fines of up to €20 million or 4 per cent of a company's turnover.

Open Europe followed up with a report in April 2016 seeking to identify deregulatory cuts that could be made after Brexit.[259] It identified three broad areas for repeal and reform: social and employment law; environment and climate change; and financial services. Its main suggestions of scrapping the Temporary Agency Work Directive and large parts of the Working Time Directive, saving just over £5 billion in employer costs a year, would seem to fall foul of May's subsequent pledge on workers' rights. The bulk of environmental savings identified were from scrapping renewables targets and also quitting the European emissions trading scheme, while financial services savings could come from ending the domestic application of the Alternative Investment Fund Managers Directive and the EU's cap on bankers' bonuses. Open Europe concluded:

There is certainly scope for deregulation outside the EU, though maybe not as large as assumed. We estimate a politically feasible deregulation agenda could lead to permanent gains of 0.7 per cent of GDP – with savings coming mostly from three areas: social employment law, environment and climate change and financial services. But even such a scenario would involve difficult choices such as scrapping renewable energy targets and deregulating social and employment laws. More broadly, the UK remains one of the most competitive developed economies, particularly in areas such as labour market, business environment and product market regulation. Yet there are of course potential gains, especially in areas such as education, skills, infrastructure and costs of certain services. There is little evidence that the EU holds us back in these areas, but their reform and the ensuing competitiveness boost will become increasingly crucial in the case of Brexit.

John Longworth, who resigned as director-general of the British Chambers of Commerce to speak out in favour of Brexit, talked of regulations costing £80 billion a year and gave a couple of examples of measures he would cut: 'People are not allowed to do overtime that they might wish to do – truck drivers tell me they are really angry they cannot do overtime,' he told a parliamentary committee in December 2016, referring to the same directive regulating driving hours targeted by Priti Patel. Longworth added that an 'ergonomic directive requires small businesses to keep a ledger of checks on the positioning of computer screens and chairs in the office … the bureaucracy surrounding that sort of stuff is a cost to business'. This may have been the Display Screen Equipment Directive of 1990, which obliged employers 'to perform an analysis of workstations in order to evaluate the safety and health conditions to which they give rise for their workers, particularly as regards possible risks to eyesight, physical problems and problems of mental stress', according to the European Agency for Health and Safety at Work.[260] An attempt to scrap this particular piece of red tape would run into the question of whether it constitutes a worker's right and is therefore protected by May's guarantee.

Another checklist for EU rules and regulations which could be amended or scrapped was drawn up in 2013 under the coalition government by its business taskforce, a group led by six businesspeople including Marc Bolland, then chief executive of Marks & Spencer, and Paul Walsh, then chief executive of Diageo.[261] Among its recommendations were exempting micro businesses (those employing nine or fewer) from EU regulations; more flexibility to disapply the Temporary Agency Work and Acquired Rights Directives; and an end to requirements for small businesses to keep written health and safety risk assessments (including the Display Screen Equipment Directive). 'European states should be free to exempt small businesses carrying out low-risk activities from the burden of record-keeping. This would benefit at least 220,000 UK small businesses, and save businesses across the EU an estimated 2.7 billion euros,' the report said. It also wanted 460,000 British small businesses freed from requirements under the Waste Framework Directive to register as waste carriers – which costs a fee – even if they only transport a small amount of their own non-hazardous waste. The Business Task Force report contained a section on barriers to innovation which highlighted the expensive bureaucracy of the EU's landmark chemicals regulation known as REACH (Registration, Evaluation, Authorisation and Restriction of Chemicals), said to be the most complex and far-reaching legislation in twenty years. This was brought in to verify the safety of chemicals on health and the environment by requiring companies to register them with an EU agency based in Helsinki. One business quoted in the Business Task Force report said: 'We've had to employ an additional four people – that's 2 per cent of our workforce – just to deal with the paperwork associated with REACH and keep us compliant.' The report added:

> The cost of registering chemicals under REACH is excessive. SMEs across the EU are hit disproportionately hard. REACH is forcing some smaller businesses to consider manufacturing outside Europe or stop manufacturing altogether. Current REACH guidance is unwieldy and complex. It forces small companies to buy in expertise to help them comply, which can cost €180 per hour. In 2018, the threshold for registration will reduce from 100 tonnes to one tonne per annum. Most SMEs will then be covered by the regime. They will have little option but to pay fees, often prohibitively high, to join 'registration' consortia to gain access to information on chemicals and register for REACH. Costs can be as high as €100,000. We have been given evidence of small firms being advised by their trade association not to grow so that they remain under the threshold.

REACH is constantly evolving, having been amended almost forty times. Chemical Watch, a specialist news service, said that if the regulation is repealed, British companies exporting to the EU might need to emulate Switzerland in appointing representatives in the EU to register their substances, incurring more red tape.[262] The publication added:

> The 'still-in-REACH' scenario would see the UK lose its ability to take part in decisions on the future of EU chemicals policy, but maintain the existing single market for chemicals, and preserve the value of REACH registrations. However, this would bring no relief to UK SMEs from the regulatory burden of REACH. The 'out-of-REACH' option, on the other hand, could potentially seriously disrupt chemicals trade. REACH implementation has been going on in the UK for almost a decade. This work would still need to continue during the interim period as a leaving member state, despite the uncertainties about the future validity of the registrations being made. The UK would then need to develop a national chemicals policy similar to REACH to address the same issues. The silver lining for the UK enterprises in the 'out-of-REACH' option would be that the other processes of REACH – authorisation, evaluation and restriction – would no longer be directly applicable to them. It might be possible to reintroduce certain substances that have been phased out in the EU.

The Business Task Force report also contained an annexe listing sixty-six EU measures which businesses wanted changed or scrapped, ranging from the Habitats Directive – covered in the Animals chapter and which seems destined for the bin based on the statements of ministers – to rules on disposing of batteries, labelling minced meat and train driver licensing. The House of Commons Library has estimated that 13.2 per cent of UK primary and secondary legislation between 1993 and 2004 was EU-related. Around 7,900 Statutory Instruments (secondary legislation) have implemented EU law while 186 Acts of Parliament (primary legislation) were in some way influenced by the EU (14.3 per cent) between 1980 and 2009.[263] According to the EU's legal website there were nearly 20,000 EU legislative acts in force at the start of 2017, including over 12,000 directly applicable EU regulations. As this book has shown, these really cover an A to Z of British life from Abattoirs (Regulation 1099/2009 on the Protection of Animals at the Time of Killing) to Zoos (Regulation 1143/2014 on Invasive Alien Species). Adding to the complication for MPs and peers, some British laws refer to EU laws or rely on definitions in EU regulations, while some domestic legislation is primarily designed to support directly applicable EU law, for example the Control of Trade of Endangered Species (Enforcement) Regulations 1997, enacted by Statutory Instrument 1997/1372 to enforce two EU regulations.[264]

The White Paper on the Great Repeal Bill published in March 2017 set out how all applicable EU rules and regulations would be converted into British law on the day after Brexit Day, timed for the end of March 2019 if the Article 50 talks went according to their two-year framework. The Bill got its name from the repeal of the European Communities Act of 1972 which gave EU law precedence over UK law – otherwise it seemed the opposite of a repealing measure. In the name of continuity, it marked a historic acceptance of thousands of European laws onto the British statute book. May said:

> We will convert the 'acquis' – that is, the body of existing EU law and its treaty provisions – into British law. When the Great Repeal Bill is given royal assent, Parliament will be free – subject to international agreements and treaties with other countries and the EU on matters such as trade – to amend, repeal and improve any law it chooses. But by converting the acquis into British law, we will give businesses and workers maximum certainty as we leave the European Union. The same rules and laws will apply to them after Brexit as they did before. Any changes in the law will have to be subject to full scrutiny and proper parliamentary debate.[265]

The process of ensuring continuity will not be straightforward, as Andrea Leadsom, the Environment Secretary, indicated in October 2016, when she told Parliament that two-thirds of applicable EU environmental law will be able to be converted with some 'technical changes' but that 'roughly a third won't'.[266] The government decided to take sweeping powers of secondary legislation known as Henry VIII powers to make 'technical' changes to British laws where they require notification to Brussels, refer to the EU in redundant ways or involve liaison with one of its forty-five agencies. The UK must decide how far to replicate the functions of these agencies, such as the European Chemical Agency in Helsinki, which ensures companies comply with the REACH regulation on the safe use of chemicals. In a few cases, such as Europol, the EU law enforcement agency based in The Hague to tackle cross-border crime and headed by a Welshman, the UK may want to continue as an associate member.

Henry VIII powers were named after the 1539 Act of Proclamations which enabled the Tudor king to legislate through proclamations enforceable in the courts. Although Henry's Act was repealed in 1547, its latter-day incarnation, the Statutory Instrument, only receives parliamentary scrutiny in some cases if an alert MP or peer requests it. A House of Commons Library report concluded that:

> Henry VIII powers are seen by their critics as transferring legislative power from Parliament to Government. This is in part because secondary legislation (also referred to as delegated legislation, subordinate legislation, or statutory instruments) generally receives less overt scrutiny in Parliament than primary legislation. As such, Henry VIII powers are often considered a means to facilitate Government to circumvent the full legislative process.[267]

It was Mark Durkan, the SDLP MP, who called the Great Repeal Bill 'the great download and save Bill', but he further asked: 'Who controls the delete key thereafter as far as these rights and key standards are concerned?' Ian Dunt warned that the Bill was well named 'because what this thing does is provide government ministers with extraordinary new powers to change or eradicate nearly half a century of law with almost no scrutiny from the press or Parliament. It is shaping up to be the single biggest executive power grab in Britain's post-war history'.[268] Lord Judge, former Lord Chief Justice of England and Wales, argued in April 2016 that the increasing use of Henry VIII powers damaged the sovereignty of Parliament and said they should only be used in a national emergency.[269] Brexit, it seems, will be just such an emergency situation and Parliament will need to be on its toes to spot if the 'technical' changes being made also throw out more substantial measures.

In March 2017, the Institute for Government, an independent think tank, said that up to fifteen new parliamentary Bills could be needed to deliver Brexit, placing a 'huge burden' on Parliament and government.[270] It said the legislation, covering areas including immigration, agriculture and customs, would leave little time for anything else, pointing out that the annual Queen's Speech typically announced about twenty new bills. It continued:

> Considerable time and resource will be soaked up and there will be precious little space left in the legislative

programme for other legislation that departments might have wanted to see pass ... Government should resist the temptation to introduce non-essential changes in the repeal bill. The priority should be on copying across the acquis, which can be amended after Brexit. The report added that 'there has been a complete lack of clarity about the role that the devolved legislatures will play in legislating for Brexit'.

The White Paper on the Great Repeal Bill published in March 2017 pledged that Westminster would 'work closely with the devolved administrations to deliver an approach that works for the whole of the United Kingdom ... what is clear is that the outcome of this process will be a significant increase in the decision-making power of each devolved administration.' In the first instance, however, it made clear that powers being repatriated from Brussels would go to the Westminster Parliament and the UK government rather than Holyrood, Cardiff and Stormont:

In areas where the devolved administrations and legislatures have competence, such as agriculture, environment and some transport issues, [they] are responsible for implementing the common policy frameworks set by the EU. At EU level, the UK Government represents the whole of the UK's interests in the process for setting those common frameworks and these also then provide common UK frameworks, including safeguarding the harmonious functioning of the UK's own single market. When the UK leaves the EU, the powers which the EU currently exercises in relation to the common frameworks will return to the UK, allowing these rules to be set here in the UK ... To provide the greatest level of legal and administrative certainty upon leaving the EU ... the Government intends to replicate the current frameworks provided by EU rules through UK legislation.

For Nicola Sturgeon, the Scottish First Minister, this was a 'power grab' by London at a time when she had won approval from the Scottish Parliament to seek a second referendum on independence and was pushing for a date. Holyrood also claimed the right to approve the Great Repeal Bill before it became law. *The Scotsman* newspaper warned that:

With the prominence that the [Great Repeal] Bill ascribes to not creating barriers within the UK, it is hard to comprehend new fishing and agriculture powers coming to the Scottish Parliament if they could conceivably lead to some of the barriers within the UK that David Davis seems so keen to avoid. Whether that amounts to a 'power grab' considering Holyrood doesn't have any of the powers currently is a matter of linguistic semantics. But David Davis would do well to ensure that not even the spectre of Westminster centralisation is allowed to gain credence, or he could find his Great Repeal Bill sunk.[271]

And what of peace – the final achievement of the Roman Empire mentioned in *Monty Python*'s famous sketch which inspired this book's title? The Pax Romana was the name given to two centuries of relative peace on the continent of Europe under Roman rule. EU member states have enjoyed a Pax Europa (overlooking terrorism and the Balkans conflict in the 1990s). The EU was awarded the Nobel Peace Prize in 2012 'for over six decades [having] contributed to the advancement of peace and reconciliation, democracy and human rights in Europe'.[272] Peace can easily be taken for granted in Europe, as David Cameron acknowledged in the speech in 2013 he used to pledge a referendum on EU membership.

> What Churchill described as the twin marauders of war and tyranny have been almost entirely banished from our continent … And while we must never take this for granted, this first purpose of the European Union – to secure peace – has been achieved and we should pay tribute to all those in the EU, alongside NATO, who made this happen.

The EU has contributed to the peace in Europe by helping the recovery of some of its member nations from dictatorship and totalitarianism. British membership was not strictly necessary for this – as Churchill himself said in his Zurich speech of 1946 when he called for a United States of Europe, Britain and its Commonwealth could be 'friends and sponsors of the new Europe' for it to succeed. During the referendum campaign,

Cameron argued it was essential for Britain to remain in the EU to prevent the Continent slipping back towards conflict. 'Can we be so sure peace and stability on our continent are assured beyond any shadow of doubt? Is that a risk worth taking? I would never be so rash to make that assumption.' Boris Johnson, responding for the Leave campaign, rejected this as fearmongering. 'No, I don't believe that leaving the EU would cause World War Three to break out on the European continent.' Cameron never mentioned World War Three but Johnson was a master at using ludicrous exaggeration to scupper his opponents. Yet as soon as the EU released its draft negotiating guidelines for Brexit talks, the fighting talk started. The EU text said that no agreement on its future relationship with the UK would apply to Gibraltar without the consent of Spain. Lord Howard, the former Conservative leader, said:

> There is no question whatever that our government will stand by Gibraltar. Thirty-five years ago this week another woman Prime Minister sent a task force halfway across the world to defend the freedom of another small group of British people against another Spanish-speaking country. I am absolutely certain our current Prime Minister will show the same resolve.[273]

In the words of Reg, leader of *Monty Python's* People's Front of Judea: 'Oh … Peace … Shut up!'

Britain was always divided over the EU. On the day the UK

joined in 1973, *The Times* published a poll which showed 38 per cent of Britons were happy at the prospect, 39 per cent unhappy and 23 per cent undecided.[274] The *Daily Mirror* published its own poll asking whether Britons wanted to see various Continental customs become commonplace. 'Pubs open all day' was rejected by three to one, while even greater margins were opposed to 'more pavement cafés', 'more shops open on Sunday' and 'coffee and a roll for breakfast, not bacon and eggs'. The only strange European habit that won a – very small – vote of approval was 'regular wine with meals'.[275] Clearly Britain has changed enormously since 1973 and become Europeanised in more ways than many would like to admit. For example, four of the country's 'Big Six' energy suppliers are European-owned – EDF (French), Scottish Power (Spanish) and E.ON and Npower (German). Although it is a myth that olive oil was only available for treating ear wax in 1973, it was not widely seen in supermarkets until the 1990s. That was the time that the single market really opened up greater competition and trade but also set the stage for the large-scale migration that helped sway voters against the EU in the 2016 referendum. *The Times* followed its 1973 poll showing a split in attitudes to Europe with an opinion article from its Brussels correspondent:

Our climate, both economic and meteorological, is unat-
tractive to most European workers. There is no reason that
many or even any will want to give up a job in, say, Holland,

to earn less money in a country with shorter holidays and
a higher unemployment rate, unfamiliar beer and a foreign
language.[276]

The economic climate, if not the meteorological one, was
transformed during forty-plus years of membership (not to
mention the beer). It is impossible to tell which of the many
developments in Britain during that period making the country wealthier, healthier and, yes, more European, would have
taken place if the UK had never joined, given the changes also
unleashed by the era of globalisation, individual mobility and
freer trade. As this book has shown, some of the big changes
facilitated by EU membership, such as VAT and unleaded
petrol, were bound to happen with or without membership
of a supranational Continental body, while others, such as
restricted working time and many environmental measures,
were by no means certain. It is instructive to look back at
attitudes four decades ago and see how much – and how little
– the political weather can change. If history is any guide,
Britain will still be divided by the European question forty
years from now.

NOTES

1   Theresa May, Brexit speech to Conservative party conference, 2 October 2016
2   http://lordashcroftpolls.com/2016/06/how-the-united-kingdom-voted-and-why/
3   Hansard, HC Deb, 7 November 2016, vol. 616, col. 1318
4   http://ukandeu.ac.uk/explainers/does-the-uk-win-or-lose-in-the-council-of-ministers/
5   https://www.collinsdictionary.com/word-lovers-blog/new/top-10-collins-words-of-the-year-2016,323,HCB.html
6   http://ukandeu.ac.uk/wp-content/uploads/2016/04/Expert-Review_EU-referendum-UK-environment.pdf, p. 6
7   https://www.cer.org.uk/sites/default/files/publications/attachments/pdf/2014/green_benefits_policy_brief_final-8767.pdf, p. 7
8   Council Directive 80/779/EEC
9   Directive 2008/50/EC of the European Parliament and of the Council
10 Council Directive 88/609/EEC and Directive 2001/80/EC of the European Parliament and of the Council
11 Directive 98/70/EC of the European Parliament and of the Council
12 http://europa.eu/rapid/press-release_MEMO-07-46_en.htm?locale=en
13 https://uk-air.DEFRA.gov.uk/assets/documents/annualreport/air_pollution_uk_2013_issue_1.pdf
14 https://consult.defra.gov.uk/airquality/draft-aq-plans/supporting_documents/Draft%20plans%20to%20improve%20air%20quality%20in%20the%20UK%20%20Overview%20document%20September%202015%20final%20version%20folder.pdf, p. 5
15 https://www.theguardian.com/environment/2017/jan/06/london-breaches-toxic-air-pollution-limit-for-2017-in-just-five-days

16   https://www.theguardian.com/business/2015/sep/22/vw-scandal-caused-nearly-1m-tonnes-of-extra-pollution-analysis-shows

17   https://www.theguardian.com/business/2016/apr/21/all-top-selling-cars-break-emissions-limits-in-real-world-tests

18   http://www.thetimes.co.uk/article/britain-faces-eu-fine-over-car-emission-scandal-8w5c6098l

19   http://www.thetimes.co.uk/article/britain-receives-final-warning-on-shame-ful-air-pollution-levels-08j6jmd6l

20   https://www.gov.uk/government/uploads/system/uploads/attachment_data/file/579200/Emissions_airpollutants_statisticalrelease_2016_final.pdf, p. 6

21   Ibid., p. 7

22   Ibid., p. 7

23   https://consult.defra.gov.uk/airquality/draft-aq-plans/supporting_documents/Draft%20plans%20to%20improve%20air%20quality%20in%20the%20UK%20%20Overview%20document%20September%202015%20final%20version%20folder.pdf, p. 4

24   https://www.theguardian.com/environment/2015/nov/18/energy-policy-shift-climate-change-amber-rudd-backburner

25   Council Directive 86/113/EEC

26   61986C0131 – Opinion of Mr Advocate General Mischo delivered on 14 October 1987. United Kingdom of Great Britain and Northern Ireland v Council of the European Communities. Minimum standards for the protection of laying hens kept in battery cages. Case 131/86

27   Council Directive 1999/74/EC

28   Treaty on the Functioning of the EU, Article 13

29   Regulation (EC) No 1223/2009

30   CJEU judgment in case C-592/14

31   Council Directive 2008/120/EC

32   CJEU judgment in case C-1/96 of 19 March 1998, paragraph 44

33   Commission Regulation (EC) No 318/2007

34   Interview with author

35   Council Regulation (EC) No 1099/2009

36   Interview with author

37   Council Directive 1999/22/EC

38   Interview with author

39   Regulation (EU) No 1143/2014

40   Council Directive 92/43/EEC

41   Council Directive 2009/147/EC

42   'Redrow boss hits out at environmental rules saying they slow up work on new homes', walesonline.co.uk, 5 December 2016

43   https://www.theguardian.com/politics/2016/may/30/brexit-spirit-crushing-green-directives-minister-george-eustice

44   http://europa.eu/rapid/press-release_IP-16-3128_en.htm

45   'Developers set for Brexit triumph over great crested newt', *Financial Times*, 10 February 2017

46   Commission Regulation (EC) 2257/94, later replaced by Commission Implementing Regulation (EU) No 1333/2011

47   Interview with author

48   Interview with author

49   Commission Regulation (EEC) No 1677/88

50   Interview with author

51   Paul Taylor, 'EU leaders to make Europe change lightbulbs', Reuters News, 9 March 2007

52   Commission Regulation (EC) No 244/2009

53   http://europa.eu/rapid/press-release_IP-08-1909_en.htm?locale=en

54   http://www.telegraph.co.uk/technology/news/5179266/Customers-buy-up-traditional-light-bulbs-before-switch-to-low-energy-alternatives.html

55   James Hall, 'Britons stock up on banned 60 watt bulbs', *Daily Telegraph*, 1 September 2011

56   Louise Randell, 'If it means I get my lightbulbs back, I want OUT', *The Sun*, 20 April 2016

57   Daniel Hannan, *Why Vote Leave*, Head of Zeus, 2016, p. xvi

58   Alice Foster, 'Ridiculous EU rules that Britain has to adhere to: six of the worst', *Daily Express*, 24 June 2016

59   'The Energy Challenge: Energy Review Report 2006', Department of Trade and Industry, CM6887, July 2006, p. 13

60   https://www.theguardian.com/environment/2006/nov/03/energy.utilities

61   'Energy guzzling light bulbs phase out to start next year', Department for Environment, Food and Rural Affairs, M2 Presswire, 27 September 2007

62   Arthur Neslen, 'Big brands "cheating" consumers with false light bulb efficiency claims', *The Guardian*, 17 December 2015

63   Arthur Neslen, 'Light bulbs excluded in EU regulations on energy efficiency claims', *The Guardian*, 12 April 2016

64   Directive 2012/27/EU of the European Parliament and of the Council

65   'UK National Energy Efficiency Action Plan', Department of Energy and Climate Change, April 2014, p. 7

66   Directive 2010/31/EU of the European Parliament and of the Council

67   'The top 100 costliest EU-derived regulations in force in the UK', Open Europe, 16 March 2015

68   Directive 2009/28/EC of the European Parliament and of the Council

69   'Renewable energy progress report', European Commission, 15 June 2015, p. 5

70   Adam Vaughan, 'Green subsidies to push UK energy bills higher than planned', *The Guardian*, 18 October 2016

71   Ben Webster, '£450 lost over failed green power programme', *The Times*, 23 February 2017

72   https://www.ons.gov.uk/economy/environmentalaccounts/datasets/ukenvironmentalgoodsandservicessectoregssestimates

73   Fiona Harvey and Juliette Jowit, 'UK opposes a 2030 renewable energy target', *The Guardian*, 11 March 2012

74   'A policy framework for climate and energy in the period from 2020 to 2030', European Commission, 22 January 2014

75   Adam Vaughan, 'UK sets ambitious new 2030s carbon target', *The Guardian*, 3 June 2016

76   Oliver Tickell, 'Leaked letter: Rudd admits 25% green energy undershoot, misled Parliament', *The Ecologist*, 9 November 2015

77   http://energydesk.greenpeace.org/2016/09/29/common-agricultural-policy-millions-eu-subsidies-go-richest-landowners/

78   http://filestore.nationalarchives.gov.uk/pdfs/small/cab-129-162-cp-36.pdf, p. 5

79   http://www.europarl.europa.eu/sides/getAllAnswers.do?reference=E-2016-005273&language=EN

80   Raoul Ruparel, Stephen Booth, Vincenzo Scarpetta, 'Where Next? A liberal, free-market guide to Brexit', Open Europe, 4/2016, p. 25

81   https://www.gov.uk/government/uploads/system/uploads/attachment_data/file/562946/fbs-businessincome-statsnotice-27oct16.pdf

82   'Agricultural subsidy reform and its implications for sustainable development: the New Zealand experience', Vangelis Vitalis, *Environmental Sciences*, 20 March 2007

83   http://www.agriland.ie/farming-news/new-zealand-dairy-cow-numbers-drop-for-the-first-time-in-9-years/#

84   http://www.freshfacts.co.nz/files/freshfacts-2015.pdf

85   Interview with author, February 2017

86   Interview with author, February 2017

87   Vrolijk, H. C. J. et al., 'Farm viability in the European Union: Assessment of the impact of changes in farm payments, LEI report 2010/11', April 2010

88   Raoul Ruparel, Stephen Booth, Vincenzo Scarpetta, 'Where Next? A liberal, free-market guide to Brexit', Open Europe, 4/2016, p. 26

89   BBC Radio 4 *Today*, 24 January 2017

90   Jan Ungoed-Thomas, 'Farm bonus for Queen', *Sunday Times*, 22 January 2017, p. 18

91   Andrew Bounds, 'Fleet decline Whitby's hopes ebb as infrastructure crumbles', *Financial Times*, 21 July 2016, p. 3

92   'British fishermen want out of the EU – here's why', UK in a Changing Europe, 14 June 2016

93   'CFP Reform – Transferable fishing concessions', ec.europa.eu/fisheries/reform/docs/tfc_en.pdf

94   Council Regulation (EEC) No 101/76

95   'UK Sea Fisheries Statistics', House of Commons Library Briefing Paper 2788, 30 November 2016, p. 4

96   Ibid., p. 5

97   Ibid., p. 10

98   Interview with author

99   Ian R. Napier, 'Fish Landings from the United Kingdom's Exclusive Economic Zone, and UK landings from the European Union's EEZ', NAFC Marine Centre at the University of the Highlands and Islands, 11 October 2016, p. i

100 Council Regulation (EEC) No 170/83

101 Judgment of the European Court of Justice Case C-221/89, 25 July 1991

102 Interview with author

103 Craig McAngus and Simon Usherwood, 'British fishermen want out of the EU – here's why', The Conversation, 10 June 2016

104 Rachel Watson, 'Scots fishing catches could double outside EU, say bosses', *Scottish Daily Mail*, 20 December 2016, p. 21

105 Daniel Boffey, 'UK fishermen may not win waters back after Brexit, memo reveals', *The Guardian*, 15 February 2017

106 Andrew Bounds, 'Fleet decline Whitby's hopes ebb as infrastructure crumbles', *Financial Times*, 21 July 2016, p. 3

107 'Review of the balance of competences between the UK and the EU Transport', HM Government, February 2014, p. 24

108 Council Regulation (EEC) No 95/93

109 Council Directive 96/67/EC and Directive 2009/12/EC of the European Parliament and of the Council

110 'Annual Statistics 1973', CAP 375, Civil Aviation Authority, August 1975

111 https://www.caa.co.uk/Data-and-analysis/UK-aviation-market/Airports/Datasets/UK-Airport-data/Airport-data-2015/

112 'The consequences of the growing European low-cost airline sector', European Parliament Policy Department, Structural and Cohesion Policies, December 2007, p. 43, http://www.europarl.europa.eu/RegData/etudes/etudes/join/2007/397234/IPOL-TRAN_ET(2007)397234_EN.pdf

113 http://www.europarl.europa.eu/atyourservice/en/displayFtu.html?ftuId=FTU_5.6.7.html

114 CJEU Judgment Case C-466/98, 2 November 2002

115 Article 43, EC Treaty

116 http://www.iata.org/whatwedo/Documents/economics/impact_of_brexit.pdf

117 Ibid.

118 Robert Wright, 'Ryanair warns about lack of Brexit urgency', *Financial Times*, 24 February 2017, p. 18

119 Paul McClean and Alex Barker, 'UK airlines brought down to earth by Brexit', *Financial Times*, 13 February 2017, p. 3

120 Graeme Paton, 'Era of falling air fares may be over, BA's owner warns', *The Times*, 25 February 2017

121 Interview with author

122 Regulation (EC) No 261/2004

123 CJEU Judgment C-12/11, 31 January 2013

124 Ryanair Holdings PLC Earnings Call, CQ-Roll Call Inc., Q3 2016, 6 February 2017

125 Hansard, HC Written Ministerial Statements, 10 December 2002, col. 11WS

126 Hansard, HC Deb, 5 June 2003, col. 364

127 Ibid., col. 362

128 http://www.independent.co.uk/news/uk/politics/brexit-eu-referendum-uk-immigration-statistics-freedom-of-movement-a7044041.html

129 https://www.gov.uk/government/uploads/system/uploads/attachment_data/file/502613/nino-registrations-adult-overseas-nationals-feb-2016.pdf

130 http://www.thetimes.co.uk/edition/comment/can-may-avoid-falling-into-the-migration-trap-f8lq6pcs3

131 House of Commons Library Briefing Paper SN 06077, 27 January 2017

132 http://www.migrationobservatory.ox.ac.uk/resources/briefings/migrants-in-the-uk-an-overview/#kp1

133 https://www.theguardian.com/commentisfree/2013/jan/28/british-dream-europe-african-citizens

134 http://www.dailymail.co.uk/news/article-2527822/A-Big-Issue-vendors-eastern-European-countries-magazines-founder-reveals.html

135 Hansard, HC Deb, 5 June 2003, col. 349

136 Directive 2004/38/EC of the European Parliament and of the Council

137 https://www.theguardian.com/uk-news/2015/jan/19/-sp-thousands-britons-claim-benefits-eu

138 http://data.parliament.uk/writtenevidence/committeeevidence.svc/evidence-document/home-affairs-committee/immigration/written/45077.pdf

139 http://www.huffingtonpost.co.uk/2014/11/05/uk-migration-ucl-study_n_6105522.html

140 https://www.migrationwatchuk.org/press-release/448

141 Statistics on recently arrived non-UK EEA nationals, HM Revenue & Customs, May 2016

142 https://www.theguardian.com/uk-news/2016/may/12/ons-short-term-migration-explains-national-insurance-gap

143 https://www.migrationwatchuk.org/press-release/448

144 http://www.bbc.com/news/uk-politics-eu-referendum-36271390

145 https://www.ons.gov.uk/peoplepopulationandcommunity/populationandmigration/internationalmigration/articles/whatinformationisthereonbritishmigrantslivingineurope/jan2017

146 NHS Hospital and Community Health Services (HCHS): All staff by nationality and main staff group in England as at 30 September 2015, Health and Social Care Information Centre

147 https://fullfact.org/immigration/immigration-and-nhs-staff/

148 http://www.bbc.co.uk/news/uk-politics-eu-referendum-36382199

149 http://www.migrationobservatory.ox.ac.uk/resources/briefings/migrants-in-the-uk-an-overview/#kp1

150 http://www.independent.co.uk/voices/brexit-theresa-may-managed-migration-article-50-single-market-access-closing-borders-there-are-ways-a7504256.html

151 https://www.border.gov.au/Trav/Work/Skil

152 https://www.theguardian.com/uk-news/2017/feb/03/brexiters-face-rude-awakening-on-immigration-warns-ex-minister

153 https://www.theguardian.com/politics/2017/mar/27/immigration-levels-will-sometimes-rise-after-brexit-says-david-davis

154 http://data.parliament.uk/writtenevidence/committeeevidence.svc/evidence-document/home-affairs-committee/immigration/written/45077.pdf

155 Tim Shipman, 'Benefits for migrants face axe', *Sunday Times*, 26 February 2017, p. 1

156 Regulation (EU) No 604/2013

157 House of Commons Written Statement (HCWS) 219, 23 January 2015

158 Council Directive 2003/9/EC and Council Directive 2005/85/EC

159 Angela Patrick, 'Mapping the Great Repeal: European law and the protection of human rights', The Thomas Paine Initiative, October 2016, p. 53

160 Council Directive 71/354/EEC and Council Directive 80/181/EEC

161 https://books.google.de/books?id=CEgJAQAAMAAJ&pg=PA32&lpg=PA32&dq=hodgson+committee+metrication+1950&source=bl&ots=Ew-

wyZXSNhz&sig=uWINdr9ZZnn--HBrKWdlhiAvBNs&hl=en&sa=X&-redir_esc=y#v=onepage&q=hodgson%20committee%20metrication%201950&f=false p. 32

162 HC Deb, 10 May 1951, vol. 487 cc. 240–1W

163 HC Deb, 24 May 1965, vol. 713 cc. 32–3W

164 Council Directive 75/106/EEC

165 Interview with author

166 Resolution of the Representatives of the Governments of the Member States of the European Communities meeting within the Council of 23 June 1981, Official Journal C 241, 19 September 1981 pp. 1–7

167 Council Directive 96/47/EC

168 Interview with author

169 Hansard, HOC Written Question 44321, 12 September 2016

170 Council Directive 75/117/EEC

171 Council Directive 76/207/EEC

172 Council Directive 79/7/EEC

173 Council Directive 86/653/EEC

174 Council Directive 92/85/EEC

175 Council Directive 96/34/EC

176 Council Directive 2010/18/EU

177 Council Directive 97/80/EC

178 Directive 2002/73/EC of the European Parliament and of the Council

179 Council Directive 2004/113/EC

180 Council Directive 77/187/EEC

181 Hansard, HC Deb, 20 July 1983, vol. 46 col. 481

182 Ibid. col. 491

183 'Women workers' rights and the risks of Brexit', TUC, 24 May 2016, pp. 3–4

184 Ibid. p. 4

185 Ibid. p. 6

186 Ibid. p. 9

187 Judgment of the European Court of Justice Case C-236/09, 1 March 2011

188 http://www.telegraph.co.uk/finance/personalfinance/insurance/motorinsurance/11521781/Men-are-still-charged-more-than-women-for-car-insurance-despite-EU-rule-change.html

189 Council Directive 93/104/EC

190 'Britain plans court challenge over limit on working week', The Scotsman, 2 June 1993

191 'Women workers' rights and the risks of Brexit', TUC, 24 May 2016, p. 11

192 Directive 2008/104/EC of the European Parliament and of the Council

193 Marina Wheeler, 'The crucial missing part of Cameron's EU deal', The Spectator, 13 February 2016

194 White Paper, 'Legislating for the United Kingdom's withdrawal from the European Union', Department for Exiting the EU, 30 March 2017, p. 18

195 https://www.liberty-human-rights.org.uk/news/press-releases-and-statements/gaping-holes-where-our-rights-should-be-libertys-analysis

196 Hansard, HC Deb, 7 November 2016, vol. 616, col. 1303

197 Ibid., col. 1311

198   Ibid., col. 1362

199   http://www.cvce.eu/content/publication/2002/6/13/341aa357-871d-4440-bc3f-a7290fc1c7a1/publishable_en.pdf

200   http://www.cvce.eu/content/publication/2005/4/7/c610eb85-fcb9-487b-8704-179006a9442f/publishable_en.pdf

201   Sir Con O'Neill, *Britain's Entry into the European Community*, Frank Cass, 2000, p. 146

202   Ibid. p. 146 and http://www.stats.govt.nz/browse_for_stats/industry_sectors/imports_and_exports/GoodsServicesTradeCountry_HOTPYeJun16.aspx

203   http://www.tradingeconomics.com/australia/exports

204   http://researchbriefings.parliament.uk/ResearchBriefing/Summary/LLN-2016-0043

205   Henry Overman and Alan Winters, 'North and South', CentrePiece, Winter 2004

206   Ibid.

207   http://ec.europa.eu/eurostat/statistics-explained/index.php/File:Real_GDP_growth,_2005%E2%80%932015_(%C2%B9)_(%25_change_compared_with_the_previous_year;_%25_per_annum)_YB16.png

208   Ibid. p. 6

209   Dominic Webb and Matthew Keep, 'In Brief: UK-EU economic relations', House of Commons Library Briefing Paper Number 06091, 13 June 2016, p. 7

210   https://fullfact.org/europe/eu-facts-behind-claims-exports/

211   http://www.civitas.org.uk/reports_articles/potential-post-brexit-tariff-costs-for-eu-uk-trade/

212   Graeme Paton, 'Motor industry must look closer to home for parts', *The Times*, 28 February 2017

213   Barry Eichengreen and Andrea Boltho, 'The Economic Impact of European Integration', Centre for Economic Policy research, May 2008, p. 1

214   Hansard, HC Deb, 6 September 2011, vol. 532, col. 609w

215   HM Treasury analysis: the long-term economic impact of EU membership and the alternatives, CM9250, April 2016, p. 6

216   Larry Elliott, 'Will each UK household be £4,300 worse off if the UK leaves the EU?', *The Guardian*, 18 April 2016

217   'Letter from America – Gingrich warms Europe against the euro', *The Times*, 21 April 1998

218   'Gingrich's mirage', *The Economist*, 23 April 1998

219   'Estimating the economic impact on the UK of a TTIP agreement between the EU and the US', Centre for Economic Policy Research, March 2013, pp. 32–3

220   Michael Gove, 'Donald Trump: Brexit will be a great thing … you were so smart to get out', *The Times*, 16 January 2017, pp. 6–7

221   https://www.youtube.com/watch?v=_cIInxTAWMo

222   'Vilsack says US–UK deal could pose fewer agricultural issues than TTIP', *Inside US Trade*, 3 March 2017, Vol. 35, No. 9

223   http://www.bbc.com/news/uk-politics-eu-referendum-35598038

224   'The Commonwealth in the Unfolding Global Trade Landscape: prospects, Priorities and Perspectives', Commonwealth Secretariat, November 2015, p. xv

225   Ibid., p. xviii

226 Ibid., p. xv

227 'Implications of the Referendum on EU Membership for the UK's Role in the World', House of Commons Foreign Affairs Committee, Fifth Report of Session 2015–16, HC 545, p. 30

228 'Unrevised Transcript of Evidence: Inquiry on the Priorities for the Commonwealth General-Secretary', House of Lords International Relations Committee, 25 July 2016, Q4

229 http://www.bbc.com/news/business-30139181

230 Directive 2009/125/EC of the European Parliament and of the Council

231 Daniel Hannan, *Why Vote Leave*, Head of Zeus, 2016, p. xvi

232 Arthur Neslen, 'EU drops plans to make toasters more energy efficient over "intrusion" fears', *The Guardian*, 8 November 2016

233 Council Directive 92/77/EEC

234 Interview with author

235 https://www.gov.uk/government/uploads/system/uploads/attachment_data/file/539194/Jun16_Receipts_NS_Bulletin_Final.pdf

236 https://www.theguardian.com/small-business-network/2016/apr/12/would-vote-brexit-help-reduce-red-tape-vat-moss-smes

237 http://news.bbc.co.uk/2/hi/uk_news/8226546.stm

238 Council Directive 76/160/EEC

239 Jack Roston, *Environmental Law for the Built Environment*, Cavendish, 2001, p. 92

240 European bathing water quality in 2015, EEA Report 9/2016, 25 May 2016, p. 26

241 Council Directive 91/271/EEC

242 'Massive water works near Winchester has "broken EU rules for 15 years"', *Hampshire Chronicle*, 8 April 2015

243 Council Directive 80/778/EEC and Council Directive 98/83/EC

244 Council Directive 91/676/EEC

245 'Exploring the relation between environmental regulation and competitiveness', SQW Consulting for DEFRA, August 2007, pp. 8 and 23

246 Directive 2000/60/EC of the European Parliament and of the Council

247 Interview with author

248 Interview with author

249 http://www.bbc.com/news/uk-england-devon-37198688

250 https://www.bloomberg.com/news/videos/2017-01-24/hsbc-s-kevin-logan-pound-is-barometer-for-brexit

251 'Economic and Fiscal Outlook – March 2017', Office for Budget Responsibility, 8 March 2017, p. 38

252 http://www.politico.eu/article/angela-merkel-no-special-treatment-for-brits-uk-brexit-eu-relationship/

253 Ian Dunt, Brexit: *What the hell happens now?*, Canbury Press, 2016, p. 160

254 Directive 2002/15/EU of the European Parliament and of the Council

255 http://openeurope.org.uk/intelligence/britain-and-the-eu/top-100-eu-rules-cost-britain-33-3bn/

256 Directive 2011/61/EU of the European Parliament and of the Council

257 'Tailoring funds regulation following Brexit', The Association of Investment Companies, November 2016, p. 6

258 Regulation (EU) 2016/279 of the European Parliament and of the Council

259   Raoul Ruparel, Stephen Booth, Vincenzo Scarpetta, 'Where Next? A liberal free-market guide to Brexit', Open Europe, April 2016

260   https://osha.europa.eu/en/legislation/directives/5

261   'Cut EU red tape: Report from the Business Taskforce', October 2013

262   https://chemicalwatch.com/47567/will-brexit-mean-avoiding-the-burden-of-reach

263   'How much legislation comes from Europe?', House of Commons Library Research Paper 10/62, 13 October 2010, p. 19

264   Jack Simson Caird, 'Legislating for Brexit: the Great Repeal Bill', House of Commons Library Briefing Paper 7793, 23 February 2017, p. 27

265   'Theresa May's Conservative conference speech on Brexit', Politics Home, 2 October 2016

266   Environmental Audit Committee Oral evidence: The Future of the Natural Environment after the EU Referendum, HC 599, 25 October 2016

267   Jack Simson Caird, 'Legislating for Brexit: the Great Repeal Bill', House of Commons Library Briefing Paper 7793, 23 February 2017, p. 36

268   http://www.politics.co.uk/blogs/2017/04/11/great-repeal-bill-anatomy-of-a-brexit-power-grab

269   Jack Simson Caird, 'Legislating for Brexit: the Great Repeal Bill', House of Commons Library Briefing Paper 7793, 23 February 2017, p. 38

270   Hannah White and Jill Rutter, 'Legislating Brexit', Institute for Government, March 2017

271   Ross McCafferty, 'Is the Great Repeal Bill a power grab by Westminster?', The Scotsman, 31 March 2017

272   http://www.nobelprize.org/nobel_prizes/peace/laureates/2012/press.html

273   Lord Howard interview on Sophy Ridge on Sunday, Sky News, 2 April 2017

274   Andy Beckett, When the Lights Went Out: Britain in the Seventies, p. 93

275   Ibid. p. 93

276   Ian Murray, 'No fear of a two-way wholesale invasion across the Channel', 3 January 1973, p. 27

GLOSSARY

Acquis Communautaire: The accumulated body of EU law from 1958, comprising all the EU's treaties and laws (directives, regulations, decisions), declarations and resolutions, international agreements and the judgments of the Court of Justice of the European Union.

Article 50: A clause in the Lisbon Treaty setting out the formal process for a member nation wishing to leave the EU, stating that a withdrawal agreement should take up to two years unless extended by unanimous agreement of all member nations.

Common Agricultural Policy: Farm support system of the EU to maintain agricultural incomes and fund rural development. Accounts for 38 per cent of EU spending, with €392 billion earmarked for the 2014–20 budget period.

Common Commercial Policy: System of EU common external tariffs, trade negotiations with third countries and internal liberalisation of trade between member nations.

Common External Tariff: Also known as Common Customs Tariff, the duty rates charged on imported goods as set out in the Common Nomenclature, which lists thousands of separate classifications for raw materials and finished products.

Common Market: A phrase from the founding Treaty of Rome described as 'a harmonious development of economic activities, a continuous and balanced expansion, an increase in stability, an accelerated raising of the standard of living and closer relations between the States belonging to it'. The name commonly used to describe the forerunner of the EU at the time Britain joined.

Council of the European Union: Forum for national ministers from different sectors to meet and take policy and legislative decisions. Based in Brussels.

Council of Europe: International human rights organisation of forty-seven nations including the twenty-eight EU members but separate from it. Founded in 1949 and based in Strasbourg, France.

Court of Justice of the EU (CJEU): Highest EU court, with supreme jurisdiction over EU policy areas. It consists of the European Court of Justice, comprising one judge from each member nation, which hears cases referred by national courts in sittings of three, five or fifteen judges; also the

General Court, which hears cases against the institutions of the EU.

Customs Union (EUCU): Removal of customs duties between EU member nations and common external approach to protect EU producers based on the Union Customs Code, which sets out data requirements and declaration procedures for exporters and importers.

European Commission: Executive body of the EU responsible for administration, oversight and proposing legislation. Based in Brussels and led by the Commission President and the College of Commissioners with one member from each EU nation.

European Convention on Human Rights (ECHR): International treaty to protect rights and freedoms drawn up by the Council of Europe and so not part of the EU. Entered into force in 1953.

European Council: EU institution where heads of government from the member nations meet regularly in Brussels to set policy goals, chaired by the Council President.

European Court of Human Rights (ECtHR): Supra-national court created by the European Convention on Human Rights to hear cases brought by individuals, groups or nations against member countries alleged to have breached civil or political rights. Based in Strasbourg with a judge from each member nation, it issues binding judgments, often including fines.

European Economic Area (EEA): Single market agreement

involving the twenty-eight EU member nations and non-EU members Iceland, Liechtenstein and Norway, where the 'four freedoms' of goods, services, capital and people apply.

European Economic Community (EEC): Forerunner of the EU created in 1957 by the Treaty of Rome, signed by six founding members – Belgium, France, Italy, Luxembourg, Netherlands and West Germany. Joined by Denmark, Ireland and the UK in 1973, it was renamed the European Community by the Maastricht Treaty in 1993 and fully incorporated into the EU in 2009 under the Lisbon Treaty.

European Free Trade Association (EFTA): Regional free trade body founded in 1960 by seven nations including the UK that were unwilling or unable to join the EEC. It had no common policies on external tariffs, agriculture or fishing. Britain left to join the EEC. Current EFTA members are Iceland, Liechtenstein, Norway and Switzerland.

European Investment Bank (EIB): Non-profit long-term lending institution of the EU said to be the world's largest public lending body. Founded in 1958 and based in Luxembourg, it loaned €77.5 billion in 2015, 90 per cent in EU countries and the rest to achieve EU goals around the world.

European Parliament: Elected EU institution for revising legislative proposals and reaching a final decision on them with the Council composed of 751 Members (MEPs), including seventy-three from the UK.

European Union (EU): Economic and political 28-nation organisation created by the Maastricht Treaty in 1993 comprising three supra-national communities (European Community, European Coal and Steel Community, European Atomic Energy Community) as well as the Common Foreign and Security Policy, and Justice and Home Affairs cooperation.

Eurozone: Nineteen-nation group of EU nations sharing the euro, which have handed monetary policy decisions to the European Central Bank, based in Frankfurt.

Lisbon Treaty: Most recent treaty amending the two treaties forming the constitutional basis of the EU (Rome and Maastricht), which came into force in 2009. Created the position of foreign envoy for the EU, known as the High Representative of the Union for Foreign Affairs and Security Policy.

Maastricht Treaty: Significant reorganisation of the EEC which came into force in 1993 to create the European Union, the single currency and the status of EU citizenship.

Qualified Majority Voting: Method of deciding contested matters in many policy areas between ministers in the Council of the EU that attaches extra weight to bigger countries in a complicated formula. Some areas such as taxation and foreign and security policy require unanimity.

Schengen: Name taken from a border town in Luxembourg for the European visa-free travel zone joined by twenty-six countries including non-EU members Iceland, Liechtenstein and Norway.

Single European Act: First major revision of the Treaty of Rome, came into force in 1987 and set out plans for the single market to begin in 1993.

Single Market: Free movement of goods, services, capital and people – the 'four freedoms' – between all EU member nations, involving the harmonisation of numerous standards and practices as well as the recognition of goods and services legally produced in member countries.

Statutory Instruments: Main method for making delegated or secondary law in the UK governed by the Statutory Instruments Act 1946. Most SIs are subject to 'negative resolution procedure', meaning they pass into law forty days after publication unless a motion is brought to annul them.

World Trade Organization: Global trade rule-setting and dispute-settling body with 164 members established in 1995 and based in Geneva, Switzerland.

ACKNOWLEDGEMENTS

I would like to thank Iain Dale and the team at Biteback for the opportunity to write this book, especially James Stephens for his belief and enthusiasm in a project to take an objective look at what the EU did for Britain, and Olivia Beattie for her sage editing. I am grateful to John Witherow, editor of *The Times*, and his predecessors James Harding and Robert Thomson for the opportunities they have given me to live and work in Brussels and Berlin as a foreign correspondent for a great newspaper. I also owe much to Richard Beeston, Roland Watson, Suzy Jagger, Jim McLean, Alistair Dawber, Imre Karacs, Claudia Komimbin, Gill Ross and David Byers in *The Times* foreign news department for their support over the years.

I have drawn on the experience of many accomplished and knowledgeable experts for the topics covered here. 'Experts' generally received a bit of a kicking during the referendum campaign and it is of course right that any one person's view should be open to question, and signs of 'group think' challenged, which I think is what Michael Gove was trying to say in his notorious TV interview attack on elite economists 'from organisations with acronyms', many of which had urged Britain to join the euro. As the smoke clears from the referendum battlefield, I would urge the general rehabilitation of the expert. None of those I spoke to were fighting old wars but were sincerely engaged with issues crucial to the future of this country. As this book has shown, the issues raised by the referendum result are often more complex than at first thought, with implications slow to emerge but nonetheless still important. So let's value our experts. We are going to need them more than ever. I would especially like to thank Stuart Anderson, Stephen Booth, David Bowles, Warwick Cairns, Leena Camadoo, Barrie Deas, Roger Douglas, Mark Gray, Inge Halstensen, Sam Lowe, Richard Murphy, Kirsten Pullen, Daniel Rosario, Peter Stevenson, John Strickland, Jim Sutton and Rachel Wyatt. I am also grateful for those who spoke to me on and off the record in the European institutions, British government, Whitehall and various groups associated with Leave and Remain. Many thanks also to colleagues in London, Brussels and Berlin who have provided ideas, insight, inspiration and support, especially Sabine Schu and Bruno Waterfield. We miss Ian Traynor and his expert coverage of all things Europe very much.

Special thanks to my family for once again putting up with

the lost evenings, ruined weekends and general social pariah status that go with writing a book about the EU. Thank you Leonard, Sheila, Mick, Gill, Liz, Ray and Mikey. Above all I am forever grateful to Michelle, Leo and Kim for making it all worthwhile.

@DavidCharter
Berlin, April 2017